Twayne's English Authors Series

Sylvia E. Bowman, *Editor*

INDIANA UNIVERSITY

John Stuart Mill

 5

John Stuart Mill

By JOHN B. ELLERY

East Tennessee State College

Twayne Publishers, Inc.   ::   New York

To:
Ellen
Thea
Martha
Sarah
Jessica
John

Preface

Even the most self-confident author could not attempt a book on John Stuart Mill without considerable trepidation. Any man who was such a mighty force in the social and economic evolution of his own country and who continues to exert immense and lasting influence on the political philosophers of all nations has naturally attracted the attention of many writers in search of a subject. The attention given to Mill, however, has tended to focus largely upon his critical sagacity as an observer of the political scene and upon the iron-clanging logic of his socio-economic theories. There seems to me to have been an unfortunate disregard for the vigor and pungent eloquence of his rhetoric. The celebrity of his many attainments notwithstanding, it is by virtue of the style and content of his written works that he stands forth as one of the most acute and distinctive writers in the literature of his period.

In this book I have attempted to delve more deeply into the fascinating miscellany of available materials by and about Mill and to present, if not brilliantly at least convincingly, a well documented full-length portrait of this incredible man. Such a critical-analytic study of his extraordinarily fascinating life and works will serve, it is hoped, to increase the appreciation for, as well as the knowledge of, the thoughts, sentiments, and hopes which inspired his writing. The great danger in such an undertaking is demonstrated in the uncritical panegyrics, on the one hand, and the theory-centered critical analyses of his postulates on the other. These judgments of Mill are without sufficient understanding of the rare spirit of the man. In order to remedy the deficiency that exists it is necessary to provide evocative insight into his great talent as a writer as well as a thinker. An essential ingredient of the remedy is the realization that he was gifted equally with genius and compassion.

It is not my intention to attempt to define anew the numerous social, ethical, political, and economic concepts enunciated by Mill in his numerous books, articles, and speeches. Nor are these pages intended to provide a compendium or digest of his ideas. Such service has been provided by scholars from various fields other than literature in a measure—a measure, as Cato would have observed, that is filled up, pressed down, and running over. Attention will be given here to such matters only when necessary to the etching of his philosophic profile. The object, simply stated, is to examine the written record and, wherever possible, to relate Mill's expressed attitudes and opinions to specific aspects of his life and time.

The Victorian era saw the growth of a democratic system of government, which had its beginning with the passage of the Reform Bill of 1832. This act, which was the most significant piece of legislation of its kind since the Magna Charta of 1215, marked the end of a general period of governmental *laissez-faire*. Middle-class liberalism was in ascendancy. The battle lines were being drawn in the class struggle between the workers and the wealthy factory owners. Social and political philosophers were converging their reflections on the economic life of the country and the great problems of humanity to which it had given birth. Only the abandonment of atrophied economic theories and the enactment of general reform could stand surety for the propriety, security, and freedom of the individual. From the background of this reform movement there emerged the strange phenomenon that was John Stuart Mill, one of the most eminent of the Victorians.

The basic problem in planning this account of Mill's life and work arises from the fact that he scattered his talent in several directions. Amid the demands of his position at India House, he found time to work on major publications, to write numerous articles for a variety of periodicals, and to edit a leading journal. In addition to his literary efforts he found intellectual stimulus in public debate, and he was a frequent speaker. While his published works received acclaim, his speeches also attracted favorable attention. His chief diversion, throughout his life, was in a change of work.

In order not to encumber the text by attempting to pursue all aspects of his various activities at one time, a strict chronological presentation has not been observed throughout. Although the main body of the text does follow the traditional chronological order, there has been some digression in the treatment of certain of his works. This was done to bring together related materials whose form, content, or significance required a unified commentary.

This arrangement, it is believed, will facilitate both reading and understanding and will provide a convenient guide for those who may wish to undertake a more intensified study of Mill's diversified career.

JOHN R. B. ELLERY

Johnson City, Tennessee
April, 1963

Acknowledgment

I should like to acknowledge my indebtedness to Louise Byron and Dr. James R. Hodges for the long hours they devoted to the manuscript, and more particularly for their advice and encouragement. I am more appreciative than these words can possibly reveal.

Special acknowledgment must be made to each of the following: G. R. C. Davis, Keeper, and K. W. Grausden, Department of Manuscripts, The British Museum; F. W. Drummond, Trustee Department, National Provincial Bank Limited, London, for information concerning the disposition of Mill's papers and documents which his department held as Executor of the late Mary Taylor; Marjorie Plant, Deputy Librarian, British Library of Political and Economic Science, University of London; David C. Means, Chief, Manuscript Division, The Library of Congress; James O. A. Ellery, for his generous assistance in translating material in the *Archiv fur Sozialwissenschaft und Sozialpolitik;* Professor George L. Nesbitt, Hamilton College; Professor Thorrel B. Fest, University of Colorado; Professor F. W. Haberman, University of Wisconsin; and the late Professor E. C. Mabie, State University of Iowa.

This expression of appreciation for the assistance I have received from those cited above at various stages of this work on John Stuart Mill does not relieve me of any responsibility for the interpretation of the material upon which this book is based. It does, however, entitle them to a full share of credit for whatever measure of success this venture may enjoy. For their sake, even more than my own, I hope that the reader will find the following pages both informative and pleasurable.

Chronology

1806   John Stuart Mill born at 12 Rodney Terrace, Pentonville, Yorkshire, England, May 20.

1809   Taken to visit Jeremy Bentham at Barrow Green and the Educational Experiment begins with John Stuart Mill as subject.

1821   Studies law with John Austin.

1822   Forms Utilitarian Society.

1823   Joins the East India Company.

1824   Publishes first articles in the *Westminster Review,* which was founded by Jeremy Bentham to be an "organ of philosophic radicalism."

1825   Edits Jeremy Bentham's *Rationale of Judicial Evidence.*

1826   Suffers from mental depression.

1828   Promoted to Assistant Examiner in India House.

1829   Delivers speech against John Sterling.

1830   Meets Harriet Taylor.

1831   Publishes *The Spirit of the Age* as a series of seven articles in the *Examiner.*

1835   Edits the *London and Westminster Review.*

1835   Burns manuscript of Thomas Carlyle's *French Revolution* by mistake.

1836   His father, James Mill, dies. Purchases *London and Westminster Review*

1837   Accession of Queen Victoria.

1843   Publishes *A System of Logic.*

1844   Publishes *Essays on Some Unsettled Questions of Political Economy.*

1848   Publishes *Principles of Political Economy.*

1851   Marries Harriet Taylor.

1853   Shows signs of consumption.

1856   Appointed Chief of the Office of the Examiner of India Correspondence.

1858   Retires from India House. Harriet Taylor Mill dies at Avignon, November 3.

1859   Publishes *On Liberty, Thoughts on Parliamentary Reform,* and *Dissertations and Discussions,* Vol. I, II.

1860   Publishes *Considerations on Representative Government.*

1863   Publishes *Utilitarianism.*

1864   Delivers tribute to William Lloyd Garrison at St. James Hall, June 29.

1865   Elected to Parliament from Westminster. Elected Lord Rector of Saint Andrews University. Publishes *An Examination of Sir William Hamilton's Philosophy* and *Auguste Comte and Positivism.*

1867   Delivers Inaugural Address at Saint Andrews, May 15. Publishes *Dissertations and Discussions,* Vol. III.

1868   Defeated in election.

1869   Publishes *The Subjection of Women,* and revision of James Mill's *Analysis of the Human Mind.*

1873   Dies at Avignon, May 7. *Autobiography* published posthumously.

1874   *Three Essays on Religion* published.

1875   *Dissertations and Discussions,* Vol. IV, published.

1907   *On Social Freedom* published.

1910   *Letters* published.

Contents

John Stuart Mill

CHAPTER 1

An Educational Experiment

THE dawn of the nineteenth century found England placid and prosperous. The landed gentry ruled with a decorum eminently proper as a prologue to the Victorian era. Business was good, and all was well with the world—or so it must have seemed to most. But, at the same time, the vast social changes brought about by the Industrial Revolution had begun to stir the social critics and militant reformers. The liberal was heard more frequently and more distinctly, and it was his voice that heralded the advent of John Stuart Mill.

James Mill, the father of John Stuart Mill, was born in 1773. He studied for the ministry at the University of Edinburgh and was licensed as a preacher in 1798. His ecumenical mission was relatively brief and unspectacular, but his philosophic zeal found expression in his espousal of the socio-economic crusade of Jeremy Bentham. As a thoroughly dedicated disciple of this messiah of Utilitarianism, James Mill directed his attention to the promulgation of the psychological explanation of Bentham's social and political theories. His greatest contribution to Utilitarianism, however, was his son.

In 1805 Mill married Harriet Burrow. The following year, May 20, 1806, their first child was born.[1] He was named after Sir John Stuart, the long-time patron and benefactor of his father. The boy was a joy to his parents and to Jeremy Bentham, who saw in him an opportunity to create an intellectual heir in his own image and likeness. Bentham had long harbored a profound contempt for the normal educational process. He could now experiment with a few educational theories of his own. And most unusual ideas they were.

Accordingly, when Mill was three years old the family was invited to visit the Bentham home at Barrow Green. James

Mill and his wife were delighted to accept, and this visit in 1809 marked the beginning of the great Educational Experiment. Between them, Mill and Bentham prepared a program of study for the youngster. Their curriculum was so austere and uncompromising that one's interest in the unique experiment is inevitably tempered with poignant overtones of sympathy for the child, and with indignation at the attitude of his tutors. Mill, fortified by a phenomenal precociousness and disciplined by a great awe of his father, appears to have reacted enthusiastically and without resistance throughout his trial.

And so it was at the age of three his formal education began. He commenced with the study of Greek and pursued this subject until he was able to translate the works of Herodotus, Xenophon, Socrates, Plato, and others with accuracy and understanding. At eight he was introduced to Latin, and went on to the works of Caesar, Vergil, Horace, Ovid, and Terence. At the same age he began the study of mathematics, which he continued through geometry, algebra, and differential calculus; the physical sciences, with particular attention given to chemistry; and English literature. With respect to the literature, he found a special source of pleasure in reading the works of Milton, Goldsmith, Burns, Spenser, and Dryden.[2]

Considerable attention was also given to Mill's training in rhetoric. He read Cicero's treatises on oratory, the *Rhetoric* of Aristotle, Quintilian's *Institutes of Oratory,* and the speeches of Demosthenes, Socrates, and Thucydides. His father required that he report daily upon the material read and that he analyze it and put it into synoptic tables as an exercise in clear thinking and verbal exposition. James Mill placed great emphasis on oral presentation, and he had John read aloud so he would develop skill in elocution. Mill tells us that his father "had thought much on the principles of the art of reading, especially the most neglected part of it, the inflection of the voice, or modulation as writers on elocution call it, and had reduced it to rules, grounded on the logical analysis of a sentence. These rules he strongly impressed upon me, and took me severely to task for every violation." [3]

The impact which his classical studies had upon him is suggested in *The Spirit of the Age,* in which he states that there can be found in Demosthenes and in "All the Athenian

orators, down to the speeches of Thucydides; Cicero and all
that we know of the Roman orators . . . keen and sagacious
observations of life and human nature, which will be prized
as long as the world shall endure." [4]

Alexander Bain provides an interesting close-up view of
Mill's early years in his account of a typical day in the youngster's life. He arose each morning at six and studied for two or
three hours before breakfast. One half hour was allowed for
this meal, which was followed by five hours of concentrated
application to his work schedule for the day. As a rule, the
more difficult assignments were reserved for the evening when,
after dinner, he returned to his studies for another two or three
hours of labor. [5] His only free time came in the late afternoon
when he engaged in peripatetic discourse with his father or
read selections from the works of those authors in whom he
had a particular interest at the moment. He was a voracious
reader, and his taste was eclectic. When he found a book that
he liked, he immediately read it through two or three times. [6]

It is difficult to accept the notion that such continuous and
diffuse intellectual activity provided unalloyed enjoyment for
the boy. There is no evidence, however, that he ever reacted
as one who was forced to endure that which he found unpleasant. His clearly manifest desire to please his father and
his possession of the necessary mental gifts apparently enabled him to find considerable personal gratification in the experience.

This course of study, or perhaps it should be called term of
apprenticeship, continued without interruption until 1820,
when he was fifteen years old. Thoroughly indoctrinated in the
Benthamite tradition and dedicated to the principle of "the
greatest happiness for the greatest number," a dictum he followed throughout his life, he now formally espoused Utilitarianism with a faith that never wavered. At the time, some
thought was given to the desirability of sending him to a university. Sir John Stuart, recognizing the boy's brilliance, had
set aside £500 in his will to provide the necessary financial
support for his namesake's university education. In spite of
this, it was concluded that such time would be wasted because a university could give Mill little knowledge he did not
already possess—or could not easily acquire on his own.

Moreover, there was some suspicion that the Cambridge professors might stultify his budding genius.

It was finally decided that he would round out his training by spending a few months in France with Jeremy Bentham's brother, Samuel. Mill enjoyed France, the country, the people, and his new friends—so much so that his visit lengthened to fourteen months before he returned to his family in England in July, 1821. The experience had been good for him; it took him away from the constant supervision of his father and gave him a chance to move and think in the rare atmosphere of personal freedom, something he had not known heretofore. He was now ready to begin the study of law, and he entered the law office of John Austin, a prominent member of the bar and close friend of his father.

James Mill joined the East India Company in 1819 as assistant to the Examiner of India Correspondence. He became Chief Examiner in 1830.

In May of 1823 John Stuart joined the East India Company as a junior clerk in his father's office. He also began serious writing; his first articles were published in the *Westminster Review,* and some of his letters appeared in the *Morning Chronicle.* His subjects ranged from freedom of the press to birth control, which is a rather broad spectrum for a seventeen-year-old mind and pen.

If Mill harbored any strong feeling of resentment against the strict regimen of his father, he was now in a position to unburden himself of some of the pressure. He made no such effort. Instead, he continued as he had in the past and applied himself assiduously to the task of advancing his knowledge. In 1822, when he had become firmly settled in his legal studies, he and a select group of young men with similar interest and intellectual drive had set about the formation of the Utilitarian Society. The organization was dedicated to study and discussion. About a dozen of these youthful reformers arranged to meet at regular intervals and, through their reading and conversation, vigorously pursued a cooperative study of a wide variety of social and political subjects in which they found a mutual interest. Among the members were William Eyton Tooke, William Ellis, George Graham, and John Roebuck.[7] The society endured for about four years and was a source of great pleasure to Mill. Interest waned, however, and the group was finally disbanded in 1826.

Part of the responsibility for the demise of the Utilitarian Society may be attributed to Mill's increasing interest in the Owenites' Cooperative Society. In 1825 he began attending the debates which were held by this organization and soon took an active part in their programs. He participated in a debate on population through five or six weekly meetings before large audiences, and he spent several additional months working on other questions considered by the group.[8]

The satisfaction which he derived from this forensic activity led him to the organization of the Speculative Debating Society, which was similar to the Speculative Society in Edinburgh in which Lord Brougham, Francis Horner, and "others first cultivated public speaking." [9] Starting in 1825 and continuing through the years of its existence, this group met once every two weeks from November to the following June. Mill opened the second debate and spoke in nearly every debate thereafter[10] until 1829 when he withdrew his membership.[11]

His experience as a debater is particularly worth noting because it paved the way for the political debates which were to follow. Mill, in his *Autobiography*, points to certain benefits which he derived from these experiences. Among other things, he learned "never to accept half solutions of difficulties as complete; never to abandon a puzzling question, but to return to it again and again, until it was manifest; never to allow obscure corners of a debated issue to remain unexplored because they did not appear to be important; never to think . . . I understood any part of a subject unless . . . I understood the whole." [12] Gustave d'Eichthal, who regarded Mill as a young man of much merit and who was a spectator at one of his debates, remarked that Mill "took up one after another all the points on which the discussion had touched, gave in a few words his opinions on these points with a restraint, good sense, and knowledge of the subject that was altogether astonishing. Never have I heard a speech in which I had less desire to change anything." [13]

I *Early Debating Society Speeches*

Mill's first speech of record, "The Utility of Knowledge," [14] was delivered at the London Debating Society in 1823, the same year in which he helped to organize this group. In it he demonstrates his implicit and, at this early age, somewhat complacent trust in his philosophical evangel. It makes explicitly clear that he had found "in learning and knowledge a creed, a doctrine, a philosophy; in one among the best senses of the word, a religion";[15] and he was already dedicated to the proposition that "it is better to be a Socrates dissatisfied than a fool satisfied." [16]

The year 1825 was a particularly productive period for his Ciceronian ambitions. He delivered three speeches on population at the London Debating Society.[17] The first two speeches, while stylistically impressive, suggest a rather inflexible adherence to the Malthusian theory of population and a somewhat conservative stand in dealing with the problem.[18] In the third and more sophisticated speech, Mill devotes his attention to the basic elements of political economy which enter into a solution of the social problems arising from the Industrial Revolution, and he considers the problems in terms of competition versus communal endeavor. The influence of the free-enterprise philosophy of Adam Smith is reflected in his criticisms of communism in industry and his arguments on the value of individual incentive and reward as essentials of progress.[19]

Somewhat later in the year he delivered a speech, "The Influence of Lawyers," [20] which successfully refutes Carlyle's accusation that he "cannot laugh with any compass," [21] with a remarkable display of tongue-in-cheek logic and apt illustration. At the same time, he reveals a microscopic ability to detect the most minute incoherence in the fabric of his opponent's reasoning. The gist of his criticism of the absurdities inherent in the legal profession is:

. . . to every cause there are two sides, and that of these one only can be right. At least one half, therefore, of a lawyer's business i deception . . . it is not easy for him, one half of whose life is spen in making the worse appear the better cause, and the other half i making the good cause appear better than it is, to retain . . . lov of truth and abhorrence of artifice and deceit without which, in my estimation at least, there can be no perfect character.

Toward the close of 1825 Mill became engaged in a debate about the British Constitution, during which he delivered two speeches.[22] In the first of these he sets forth the thesis that a constitution is good only insofar as it serves its true function: providing a good government. The test of good government is the prosperity of the country as a whole. Proceeding from these basic assumptions, he attempts to show how men commonly err by attributing prosperity to the whole country when actually only the aristocracy are prosperous. Prosperity is valid only when it applies to all of the people and not to just a select group. The speech is, however, less of a diatribe against the aristocracy as a class and more of an indictment of the governmental system which permitted such a class to attain a position of power. As such, the speech is essentially an argument for popular government, and it presents the basic political philosophy which is the central theme for his later speeches in Parliament on the Reform Bill.

The second speech on the constitution typifies Mill's youthful felicity of phrase and illustration. At times his resentment of the hedonism of the aristocracy excites him to a point where the young-Mephistophelian atmosphere[23] which surrounds some of his earlier Debating Society speeches is dispelled. And as he attacks the control exercised by the aristocratic ruling clique over the thoughts and actions of other individuals, one senses an embryonic form of *On Liberty*.

Reading the speech one tends to be first irritated, then amused, and finally impressed. It is shocking, perhaps, to find Mill stating that "the bulk of the people at least who have arrived at the age of manhood are stupid, obstinate and ignorant." The effect is even more disconcerting when he declares that "we must resign ourselves to be governed by incapables of some sort." But his principle begins to come into proper focus when he adds that "it is better to be governed by an incapable people rather than an incapable aristocracy" because the people are honest, sincere, genuinely interested, and willing to learn.

It is a truism that every philosophy has areas of vulnerability. One is reminded of this in Mill's speech, "The Influence of the Aristocracy," presented at the London Debating Society, on December 9, 1825.[24] In this particular speech he implies that equality of rights does not presuppose equality of ability. At the same time, probably because of the influence of Comte and the Saint-Simonian school with which Mill was to become intimately associated, he gives an aristocratic tinge to his theories of democracy by suggesting the necessity of obedience to the expert. Mill becomes rather mordant in his criticism of the idle rich for their hedonistic existence, and, at the same time, he promotes a working aristocracy that is almost as far removed from democracy.

The political developments of 1827 provided the incentive for Mill's next major forensic engagement. Early in the year, Lord Liverpool retired as Prime Minister because of poor health. George Canning, a prominent Tory, was summoned by George IV to form a new government. Canning's sympathy for the Roman Catholics, however, cost him the support of many prominent members of his own party, including the Duke of Wellington and Sir Robert Peel. Both declined to serve with him, and his only recourse was to solicit support from the Whigs. The result was a coalition government made up of loyal Tories and moderate Whigs. A few months later Canning died. He was succeeded in office by Frederic Robinson, Viscount Goderich, who subsequently resigned in 1828 and was in turn succeeded by Wellington.

Mill delivered his speech, "The Coalition Government," at the London Debating Society.[25] He is moderate in his remarks and refrains from making any final judgment; he maintains only that "the coincidence of opinion which ought to be required in a ministry is not absolute coincidence; it is sufficient if they coincide more nearly with one another than any part of them do with their common opponents."

· Following this he presented to the same group his more philosophic address, "Perfectibility." [26] In seeking to answer the general question of whether or not mankind is capable of improvement, he concentrated upon moral improvement in particular. He maintained that a virtuous life can be attained and that mankind can move in the direction of perfection. According to his reasoning, since there have been virtuous men, there must be causes that made them so. The problem is to find this causal relationship. If these causes, whatever they may be, have acted on some men, they "can be made to act upon all mankind, or the greatest part." Consequently, "it is within the power of human exertion to make all or most men as virtuous" as those upon whom these causes have already acted. The manner in which he treats his subject has led Elie Halevy[27] to describe Mill as one "who united the wisdom of an old man with the simple enthusiasm proper to a youth."

There are but two more speeches in the recorded chronology of Mill's activity in the London Debating Society.[28] Delivered in 1829, both are of particular importance in arriving at a true evaluation of his intellectual orientation at this period in his life. Of these, the first, which placed Mill in opposition to John Sterling,[29] is a defense of Bentham's opinions against the tenets of Montesquieu.[30] In it Mill sets forth this belief: "The one great principle of Bentham's system was that the body which holds the governing power should be chosen by and accountable to some portion or other of the people whose interest is not materially different from that of the whole." [31]

The second of these speeches, "On the Church," [32] treated the basic question of whether or not the Church of England was guilty of unchristian conduct. The Church of England had persecuted dissenters, had become part of the system of patronage by making choice clerical appointments available to influential members of the aristocracy, and seemed to have lost the essential spirit of Christianity. Mill, while not a religious man in any traditional sense, was a great admirer of Christian ethics. Consequently, he assailed the Church for having assumed a position of power, a position made possible through the enactment of prejudicial and discriminatory acts of Parliament. The Church had, in the process, reached a point where it now believed that "The word of God was not fit to be read unless that of a man was administered along with it, and their account of what God said, or what in their opinion He should have said, was to be forced down the throats of babes and sucklings avowedly on the ground that unless a belief in it were firmly fixed in the mind at an age previous to that at which the reasoning faculty begins to operate, in all probability the habit would never establish itself at all."

II *Mental Crisis*

As he entered his nineteenth year, Mill should have paused and taken inventory of his many activities. It might have enabled him to avoid the mental storm that was brewing. Unfortunately, no such idea presented itself to him.

In addition to his regular responsibilities at India House, he maintained a heavy writing schedule, including a number of articles for the *Westminster Review* and for the *Parliamentary History and Review*. A more ambitious and exhausting task was his editing of Jeremy Bentham's *Rationale of Judicial Evidence*. At the same time, Mill organized the Utilitarian Society, founded a debating society, and played an active part in both. The few remaining hours of each day were largely devoted to his usual task of serving as tutor for his several brothers and sisters and to the continuation of his law studies. This impossible program went on without any significant variations in character or degree through 1825 and into the following year. Then, in May, this mighty intellectual structure began to tremble under the unceasing strain.

The stress of his rigorous program and the magnitude of the demands that were continually made upon his teeming brain at long last brought Mill to the breaking point. It was more than even he could bear; and, as he reports in the *Autobiography,* he finally posed an unusual question for himself:[33] "Suppose that all your objects in life were realized; that all the changes in institutions and opinions which you are looking forward to could be effected at this instant; would this be a great joy and happiness to you?" And his shattering answer to his own question—*No!*

He continued to vex his mind with many difficult and sometimes insoluble problems, but with growing weariness of spirit. A feeling of unworthiness began to manifest itself, and this gradually led to a strange sense of spiritual isolation. There was no one to whom he might turn for sympathy or understanding, no one to whom he could reveal his anguish and distress. His reasoning became stilted by disturbing thoughts, by fear and apprehension; his mental agitation slipped into apathy and then into despondency. Somehow, calling upon some deep and strange well of strength, he managed to pull himself out of his mental depression and back to normalcy. The experience left its unalterable marks: a new and stronger man arose from the ashes of a fevered youth.

A. W. Levi, in his case study of Mill's mental crisis, maintains that "the real cause . . . was those repressed death wishes against his father, the vague and unarticulated guilt which he had in consequence, and the latent, though still present, dread that never now should he be free of his father's domination." [34] There is no doubt that the relationship between father and son was marked by great respect rather than warm affection. It may well be that Mill did resent his father. On the other hand, he had never shown any fear of expressing himself directly and forthrightly when circumstances demanded; and he subsequently demonstrated his willingness to beard this crusty old lion in his den when his romance with Harriet Taylor became a point of serious disagreement.

In the light of other evidence, however, there seems good reason to believe that the factors involved in his mental crisis were: first, fatigue approaching exhaustion; second, an uneasiness and uncertainty resulting from the fact that his reasoning was leading him to question beliefs in which he had previously felt secure, and upon which he had established the authority of his father and Jeremy Bentham. Running deep in this sad and unpleasant experience was the growing realization that his father did not know all of the answers and could be wrong. In Mill's case, he expected more; and he suffered more as a consequence. Had he been of weaker fiber the results might have been disastrous. Fortunately, his intense vitality sustained him. His self-examination was conducted with surgical precision, and he discovered the source of his problem. For a time, his spirits continued low, but the hours of dejection gradually diminished. His manner thereafter was much less deferential toward the old gods, and he set out to create his own realm of philosophy.

At first his state of mind made literary work impossible. Over the next two or three years he resumed his forensic activities and worked on a variety of articles. His search for intellectual companionship led him to a group of loyal and admiring friends and the resultant pleasures of social intercourse. By 1830 there was scarcely a trace of his prolonged mental struggle.

III *Harriet Taylor*

Up to this point Mill's life was devoid of romantic interest; study had been the controlling force in his life. Then in 1830 he met Harriet Taylor at a dinner party. The equivocal, if not definitely illicit, relationship which followed would have caused talk in any age. It is not difficult, therefore, to appreciate the reaction of Victorian society.

He was, at this time, twenty-four, and his star had been incessantly ascendant. Now, however, he was brought face to face with public opinion in an area in which he was perhaps least qualified to defend himself. Indeed, it is difficult to discover any suitable defense available to him. Mrs. Taylor was twenty-three, married, the wife of a fine gentleman, and the mother of two children. There is no evidence of dissatisfaction with her marriage until her affair with Mill. Be that as it may, the romance blossomed despite the obstacles provided by husband, home, and family; and Mill was no longer forced to turn to his work for solace in lonely hours.

Throughout his life, moral or intellectual errancy was anathema to Mill. His thoughts and actions were the very embodiment of ethical practicality. Consequently, his affair with Harriet Taylor, a self-indulgence to such an extreme that all standards of prudence were disregarded, was so uncharacteristic that it is not easy to understand. If there is any explanation, it can only be found in his moral and spiritual value structure —one that was peculiar, but not without precedence in moral philosophy.

Although there is no known photograph of Mill in these early years, excellent descriptions of him are to be found in the letters and memoirs of friends and acquaintances. Carlyle described him at about this time as a slender, rather tall and elegant youth; and he remarked about Mill's earnestly smiling eyes.[35] Courtney, who was impressed by his slim figure and his youthful face, describes him as having fair hair and a ruddy complexion;[36] Bain adds the observation that his features were expressive, without aiming at strong effects.[37] There seems to be no doubt that he was an attractive looking man.

Jane Welsh Carlyle was moved to comment in a letter to her cousin, Helen Welsh, that "among all the literary people that come about us the one I like best is Mr. Mill." [38] In any case, Harriet Taylor found him very attractive; and, according to Carlyle, she found her husband very dull. The great romance contained, therefore, all of the traditional elements of the eternal triangle—the dull but devoted husband, the beautiful but bored wife, the gallant but gullible lover. It may be difficult to visualize Mill in the latter role, but it was actually what might have been expected. His unusual childhood—the isolation imposed upon him first by his father and later by his own preoccupation with intellectual matters, the absence of anyone to whom he might turn for love and understanding—these combined to make him a prime subject for the attentions of an attractive, intelligent woman.

The timing was perfect. Mill was young, handsome, and a man of some importance. He had been promoted to a superior post in India House in 1828, and he had already established himself as a literary figure of more than ordinary stature. Mrs. Taylor, according to Mill, had: "Married at an early age, to a most upright brave and honorable man, of liberal opinions and good education, but without the intellectual or artistic tastes which would have made him a companion for her. . . ." [39] Others saw her in a less flattering light. To them, she appeared to be a coquette who wanted more than the quiet security of her home and who saw in Mill the intellectual Caesar to whom she might be Cleopatra and thereby bask in the reflected glory of his social and cultural recognition.

The friendship grew gradually; but the roots ran deep. At first there were casual conversations and very proper epistles. Soon there were clandestine meetings and passionate letters. Mill's visits to the Taylor home became so frequent that he was spending virtually all of his free hours there. John Taylor, a much too amiable man, eventually realized that this affair was more than a mere friendship. Although he attempted to persuade his wife that her association with Mill had assumed improper proportions, she remained adamant. For a time he accepted the situation, remained placidly in the background, and hoped that a change of heart or the pressure of public opinion would restore his wife to him.

Time changed nothing for the better. There was a feeble attempt at maintaining the outward appearance of a normal family life, but John Taylor carried most of the burden. His efforts were in vain. Their friends and acquaintances knew what was happening. John Roebuck, convinced that his long and close friendship with Mill demanded that he intercede, visited Mill at India House and attempted to persuade him to end the affair. Mill rejected the advice and repudiated their friendship. The break was never repaired.[40] Eventually the pressure of public censure did make itself felt, however, and the two appeared in public only infrequently. The result was that they spent more time together in private.

Early in 1833 John Taylor made one more attempt to bring his wife to her senses. He suggested a trial separation for six months. His fond hope was that this would give her the time and the opportunity to realize the error of her ways. He was confident that she would return to her home with renewed love and devotion. He was wrong.

Mill was equally confident. He hoped that Mrs. Taylor would make the final break and seek a divorce. He, too, was wrong. It might have been that she still felt a certain affection for her husband, or it might have been concern for her children; it was probably fear of the notoriety which divorce necessarily entailed. Whatever the reason, divorce was not the answer.[41] Mrs. Taylor went to France, Mill followed, and everything continued as it had been. They remained, as Jane Carlyle noted in a letter to John Sterling, "ecstatically moony." [42] John Taylor continued his hopeless search for a solution until July 18, 1849, when he died of cancer. If his death was a release for his wife, it was also a long-deserved escape for him. For almost twenty years he had had to endure a situation that was anathema to his moral and ethical sensibilities. Mill assisted Mrs. Taylor in matters relating to the burial but did not attend the funeral.

The problems surrounding their relationship were not immediately resolved. Their relationship had been so obvious and so intimate that an immediate marriage would have served only to provoke the most offensive gossip. Moreover, convention demanded a respectable period of mourning for the deceased; and Harriet Taylor, for all of her liberal views, lacked the courage and fortitude to undertake this breach of propriety. Consequently, the romance continued very much as it had until August 21, 1851, when they were married in a quiet civil ceremony.[43]

IV *Code of Ethics*

How can we reconcile the questionable morality of this adventure with the strict code of ethics that dominated all other aspects of Mill's life? If there is any answer to this paradox it must reside in his concept of God, religion, and the good life. And few aspects of biography are more difficult and dangerous than those that assess another's spiritual life. The observer must rely upon the expressed beliefs and manifest virtues of his subject. When the natural difficulties inherent in such a situation have superimposed upon them the screen of subjective evaluation, the conclusions drawn are likely to appear presumptuous. On the other hand, there is a measure of truth in the belief that virtue will find expression and that it can be recognized. In the case of Mill, some attempt at the identification of moral values, if undertaken with judiciousness and charity, seems reasonable and proper.

The qualities of mind and character that fostered Mill's recognition of his obligation to society confirmed his belief that he was the proper guardian of his own spiritual well-being. He had little sympathy for metaphysical speculation. Consequently, he understood the formulation of his own theological concepts just as he did the formulation of his political or economic theories. Despite, or perhaps because of, the arduousness of this exercise in theology in terms of the demands made upon his intuition and resourcefulness, he seems to have found it an exhilarating experience. He discovered in the realm of religious dogma a pleasurable excitement induced by the struggle with ideas and an acute delight in the challenge it provided for his highly developed sensibilities.

As might be expected, he was incapable of emotional surrender to or adulation of the more ritualistic elements of any established church. This did not prevent him from feeling a genuine respect for Christian ethics that were clearly distinguishable in their social implications and associations. In religion, as in politics, he was a Utilitarian who could support any affirmative effort that might exert a positive influence. It seemed to him that a comparatively high proportion of Christian beliefs could provide effective assistance in hastening the process and in advancing the cause of liberty for the individual. But he also found a great deal of superstition mixed with Christian truths.

Just as the severe regimen of instruction devised by his father and Jeremy Bentham provided the mold in which Mill's intellect was cast, so the strict moral discipline of his paternal home provided the fine etching for his spiritual values. His concept of religion as the relationship of the individual to certain spiritual influences moves along entirely direct and logical lines to conviction—not a concept rooted in tradition, but one confirmed by self-examination and reason.

Mill was not a philosophical skeptic where religion was concerned. He was, rather, "one who had not thrown off religious belief, but never had it." [44] This assertion was not intended to serve as a disclaimer of moral responsibility. His fundamental assumptions concerning the adequacy and potency of reason, however, required that he suspend judgment with regard to certain aspects of established religion. Prudence, justice, and charity provided the wellspring of his theology.

"In regard to religion," he observed, "I do not think it right either to teach or to allow anyone else to teach authoritatively, anything whatever that one does not from the bottom of one's heart and by the clearest light of one's reason believe to be true." [45] This view was not presented as a challenge to organized religion. Although his was an affirmative philosophy which demanded that accepted principles be affirmed by reason, Mill did not hesitate to admit the possibility of the existence of God. "In the present state of our knowledge," he tells us, "the adaptations in nature afford a large balance of probability in favor of creation by intelligence. It is equally certain that this is no more than a probability, and that the various other arguments of natural theology which we have

An Educational Experiment

considered add nothing to its force. Whatever ground there is, revelation apart, to believe in an author of nature is derived from the appearance of the universe." [46]

These observations were not embellished with adventitious estimates of the exact nature of God. Mill was incapable, however, of accepting the paradox suggested by a God possessing an egotistical consciousness of power which required a haughty imposition of His own will and which ordained evil for the sake of salvation. He echoed the sentiments of his father concerning the existence of an omnipotent and benevolent God: "He found it impossible to believe that a world so full of evil was the work of an author combining infinite power with perfect goodness and righteousness." [47] Nevertheless, the relationship of Mill's ethics to religion is not particularly difficult to establish if one remembers that by religion he means the relationship of the individual to moral and ethical influences. The logical consequence is, on the one hand, a distinct unity of purpose, and a suggestion that there are as many religions as there are individuals, on the other.

Although he may at times seem to have repudiated the whole tradition of Christian belief, his frankness can well be taken as proof of his freedom from antireligious prejudice. He was neither diffident nor assertive concerning Jesus Christ, whom he placed "in the very first rank of the men of sublime genius," and who came upon the earth with "a special, express and unique commission from God to lead mankind to truth and virtue." [48] Mill's object was to remove illusions in order to better examine ideas as a source of insight into eternal truths. Theology, it seemed to him, too often sought to explain natural phenomena by attributing them to supernatural forces. The resultant body of religious beliefs was much too chaotic to satisfy his reflective mind. So much depended upon faith, and he could never accept blind faith as a logical source of wisdom or as a basis for a true, profound understanding of the realities of life. He could never be a convinced theist; he never wanted to be.

It was Mill's firm belief that a life dedicated to truth and virtue could be achieved independently of religious ritual and dogma, the showpieces of religion. A life so dedicated is a moral one, and morality demands the rigorous honesty of philosophical empiricism, arising from an awareness that ideas of morality and justice are influenced by economic and social conditions. Most significant is the fact that few actions proceed from instinctive sources, for the primary stimulus of human behavior is purposeful striving based on an individual's set of values. Thus ethics becomes a matter of individual initiative and responsibility. Around this concept of human morality, Mill formed a coherent system of personal ideals which he pursued, with one possible exception, throughout his life. To Mill, there was not even that one exception. Bentham had taught him well that each man knows what is best for himself.

V A Woman's Influence

There is, of course, no question that the affair between Mill and Harriet Taylor was the subject of great controversy, and that the imputations of wrongdoing endowed it with generally derogatory connotations. It is also true, however, that only the participants had a full and exact knowledge of the association; no other may claim to have a clear and true conception adequate to a proper judgment. On the other hand, there is less chance of misjudging the effect that Harriet Taylor had upon Mill. In his *Autobiography* he describes her beauty, charm, and wit in most eloquent terms.[49] He discourses at great length on her moral character, her powers of discernment and eloquence, her penetrating and intuitive intelligence, her genius.

It would seem that he was prejudiced. The evidence available, particularly Mrs. Taylor's correspondence with Mill, would seem to indicate that she was not endowed with an intellect quite so rare as her ardent admirer would have us believe.[50] Her philosophic reflections suggest a quickness in apprehension rather than a fullness of comprehension.

In any event, she did have a clearly manifest influence on Mill, if only because her presence was a strange but potent inspiration. He repeatedly comments on his intellectual indebtedness to her. The Preface to *Dissertations and Discussions* pointedly acknowledges her substantial contribution, the *Principles of Political Economy* is presented as a joint production, and she is even given a measure of credit for *A System of Logic*.[51] There is, in fact, little doubt that everything Mill published after 1843 reflected, to some degree, her attitudes and opinions. Harriet Taylor seems to have had a penchant for expressing her views on the slightest provocation, and she seemingly was driven by ambitions to have them immortalized in print. Mill could do this for her, and in return she imparted a warmth and an affection which were apparently essential to his mental and physical well-being. Either the strength of her conviction or the force of her personality established her power over him, and she was very much aware of the fact.

VI *Author, Editor*

Although the great romance provided a wonderful subject for conversation, it was not the most important event of the day. Among other things, there was the July Revolution in France. Charles X, in one of his less brilliant political maneuvers, issued the celebrated "four ordinances" which, among other things, suspended liberty of the press, restricted the franchise to landowners, and in general angered the people. He signed the decrees on July 25, 1830. By July 27, when his people had understood what he had done, the riots started. Two days later the army had been driven out of Paris, and Louis Philippe, the "Citizen King," was on the throne. The expectations were that he would be a liberal monarch; and, when he took up his scepter, Mill took up his pen. The economic crises and constant disturbances in France touched many of his political theories, and he wrote copiously in the newspapers.

The first major product of Mill's new literary inspiration was *The Spirit of the Age,* which was originally published as a series of seven articles in the *Examiner.* In attempting his analysis of the character of the times, he stressed his adherence to the Comte-Saint Simon philosophy of history. Perhaps the most unexpected aspect of his credo was his assertion concerning the value of the enlightened despotism of a knowledgeable ruler. It seemed both natural and proper for the masses to be governed by someone who knew how to take care of them. Conversely, it seemed to him completely unnatural and improper for those who did not know how to take care of themselves and protect their own rights to exercise authority.

Though his preparation was as methodical as ever, the intellectual results were disappointing. The attempt to equate this position with the Benthamite Utilitarian tradition of accepting each man as the best judge of his own interests was absurd. Mill's plea for social revolution as the ultimate solution to class struggle has the appearance of Communist doctrine and was essentially Utopian nonsense.

The Spirit of the Age missed fire, and Mill was later to feel very much ashamed of it. If any achievement can be credited to the enterprise, it can only be the fact that it brought Mill and Thomas Carlyle together. The latter, after reading the essays in the Examiner, set out to locate the author. This overture marked the beginning of a cordial friendship that covered a span of many years and endured some grievous trials and tribulations. Though the two men did not spend a great deal of time together, they did engage in an extensive exchange of correspondence.

So the third decade of the nineteenth century started for Mill with a walking tour and ended in a mad race to meet publication deadlines. He worked on his books, published dozens of pamphlets, and flooded editors with articles, essays, and letters. It is often forgotten that he accomplished all this while holding down a responsible position in industry, tutoring his eight brothers and sisters, assisting his father and Jeremy Bentham, and serving as Harriet Taylor's alter ego. The difficulties which beset him were imposing.

His five essays on Some Unsettled Questions of Political Economy were composed during 1830 and 1831 and revised somewhat in 1833. Although they were published as a volume in 1844, these commentaries can scarcely be regarded as forming a major work. They do serve, however, to reveal the emergence of a theoretical profile which was to assume a more distinct identity in his Principles of Political Economy. He also prepared a critical explanation of Jeremy Bentham's philosophy for Sir Edward Bulwer's England and the English.

While writing these essays, Mill was also a regular contributor to the Monthly Repository in which John Taylor had a financial interest and in which a variety of poems, book reviews, and articles by Mrs. Taylor appeared. As a matter of fact, insofar as can be determined, the Repository was the only journal in which anything bearing her name was published. Moreover, everything she published appeared in print in a single year—1832. Her style reflects Mill's influence, and there were some who at the time suspected that his contribution to her efforts may have been more tangible than inspirational.

As an interesting sidelight to his main interest, Mill focused his critical attention on poetry, and wrote some fairly acute, though somewhat dogmatic, criticisms. During his period of mental unrest, he had read Wordsworth's poetry, and he asserted that it had shown him "the happiness to be found in tranquil contemplation." [52] With Mrs. Taylor's encouragement, he developed an appreciation and affection for Shelley. He disapproved of Byron "because of his adverse effect on character," and gentle Browning was held suspect. The works of Scott and Coleridge, however, were looked upon as pure poetic genius.[53] There was not a great amount of time and effort devoted to this literary criticism, which is perhaps just as well. It was an interesting change of pace from political theory and economics, but that is about all that can be said for it. Mill lacked the sensitivity and perspective essential to sophisticated literary criticism.

In 1835 Mill moved through an amazing writing schedule at a formidable pace. He began editing the *London Review,* which was to merge with the *Westminster Review* the following year. Added to this, he continued his work for the *Examiner,* composed several articles for *Tait's Magazine,* and produced a lengthy technical discourse on property laws for the *Jurist,* a legal journal. Unfortunately, what started out to be a promising and productive year developed into one with more than an ordinary share of tribulations.

First, tragedy in a most unusual form introduced itself with startling suddenness. Thomas Carlyle had spent long years accumulating material for his monumental treatise, the *French Revolution.* Having suffered through the agonies of scholarly authorship, he finally completed the first volume of this massive work and asked Mill to read the manuscript before it went to the publisher. Mill was delighted with this gesture of friendship and respect. He took the manuscript to his father's home, where he normally pursued his own literary efforts. Carlyle, in an understandable but unwise spirit of exultation, celebrated his achievement by destroying the rough notes over which he had labored for so long. It was a time for celebration.

Some time later, Mill was cleaning his room and decided to burn an assortment of miscellaneous newspapers and literary impedimenta that had accumulated on his desk. Having completed this housekeeping chore, he turned his attention to his friend's manuscript. Then the horror of what had happened struck him. A frantic search by the distraught Mill and by the household servants left no room for the slightest doubt: Carlyle's manuscript had been reduced to a heap of ashes on the hearth.

He immediately rushed to the home of his friend to tell him the terrible news. Carlyle, who had been exhausted by his long labor, somehow managed to remain charitable and sympathetic. He soothed Mill and sent him on his way; then he went back to work and spent the next five months rewriting his book. There is no evidence that he ever permitted this heartbreaking experience to alter his affection for Mill. It is worth noting, however, that he never again asked Mill to read a manuscript. Both men had learned a painful lesson.

There were other developments, much less dramatic but much more important, in store for Mill. He was still his father's acolyte; his own writing served to limn the thoughts of Jeremy Bentham. Now his education, his period of apprenticeship was drawing to a close. The death of his father and the assumption of major literary responsibilities marked the end of the great educational experiment.

James Mill, who had been in declining health through 1835, died on June 23, 1836. Mill's comments on his father's death in the *Autobiography* manifest great respect, but they do not reveal any appreciable measure of filial affection.[54] Mill clearly regarded his father as an eminent man of letters and as a prominent figure in the history of political science. Although James Mill had been a strong and brave man, his leadership of the intellectual radicals removed him from the spirit of the times. As a result, he had failed to receive the recognition and praise which were rightfully his. Acknowledging all this, Mill's final assessment of his father's intellectual worth was that he had been an outstanding and original thinker, but quite definitely inferior to Jeremy Bentham. The penetrating objectivity of this evaluation suggests that he may have believed that the father was also inferior to the son.

In 1837 Mill became the sole proprietor of the *London and Westminster Review,* which he had been editing since the merger in 1836. He also resumed writing on *A System of Logic,* a work that had lain dormant for several years. Two books had been completed earlier, and a third was finished in 1838. But even all of this work was not quite enough to keep him busy and out of trouble. This same year he joined a group that became involved in a scandal of sorts.[55] It was a sorry sequel to the Harriet Taylor affair.

During the summer of 1838 John Sterling organized an informal club, originally called the Anonymous Club and subsequently named the Sterling Club. The object was to provide a meeting place where his little coterie of friends could get together, usually once a month, and socialize. According to Mill's account of their activities, in a letter to Harriet Taylor,[56] there were only twelve to twenty members at the start, but this number greatly increased in due course. No precise organizational structure was established, and no dues were paid. These gentlemen simply agreed to get together from time to time, more or less as the spirit moved them, for dinner and congenial companionship.

Some time later, the *Record,* a newspaper, discovered a list of the members, and it noted that infidels such as Mill and churchmen such as Bishop Thirlwall and Wilberforce were included. This suggested a most unholy alliance of the blessed and the damned. Mill describes what followed in his letter to Mrs. Taylor: ". . . combining this with Hare's *Life of Sterling,* it charges Hare, Maurice, French, these bishops, and innumerable others with founding a society to honour and commemorate an infidel—and joining for that purpose with persons strongly suspected of being no better than infidels themselves, such as Carlyle and me."

The basis of the attack, which reached its climax in 1844, was the fact that Hare was a dignitary of the Anglican Church and Sterling had abandoned the faith. When Sterling died [57] and Hare assumed the responsibility for editing his unfinished literary works, the cries of outrage from the righteous knew no bounds. The associations with two such freethinking stalwarts as Mill and Carlyle simply added highly combustible fuel to the incendiary blast. Mill was eager to defend Sterling's honor and reputation, but he was cautioned against making matters worse by his participation. It was not until Carlyle published his biography of Sterling in 1851 that matters were set straight.[58]

This unpleasant experience had no serious or lasting effect on Mill, and it is worth relating only because it indicates something of the public image of Mill and certain of his acquaintances.

CHAPTER 2

From Logic to Liberty

THE 1840's began quietly enough for most Englishmen. England was very much devoted to the task of bringing modern civilization to ancient China and, coincidentally, developed a profitable traffic in opium in the process. This eventually led to the Opium War, which was no great problem for the troops in Her Majesty's Service. When the dust settled, Hong Kong had become a Crown Colony, and was destined to serve as a convenient wholesale outlet for the laudanum trade. Among other things, the population of London reached the two million mark, and a British garrison was ambushed and massacred somewhere in India. It was a typical Victorian year.

Meanwhile, in 1841 Mill wrote his last two articles for the *London and Westminster Review.* The first was a gentle but discerning discussion of the errors and deficiencies of Bentham; the second was an article on Coleridge. Both were interesting; neither was particularly conspicuous for any massive contribution to the advancement of Western culture.

Then, after six years of editing and publishing the *Review,* a task that had occupied a major portion of his free time, he decided to sell the journal. By this time, he had more ambitious projects in mind and could ill afford the demands made upon him by his editorial responsibilities. In the *Autobiography*[1] he says that his mental attitudes had been fully developed and that there were no subsequent changes in his basic beliefs. Consequently, he was ready to set down on paper a definitive account of his views about a wide range of subjects. The pen, which he took up at this time, would scarcely rest for the next thirty years.

With all the loose ends of his various literary activities drawn together and with his social affairs as much under control as possible in his peculiar circumstances, Mill could clear his desk for another writing chore of real magnitude: his *Principles of Political Economy*. Now thirty-five years of age, he was already a man of stature and importance in literature, philosophy, economics, and political science. As a matter of fact, in 1841 he was virtually the elder statesman of the world of letters inhabited by some of the greatest names of Victorian literature. Charles Dickens and Robert Browning were each twenty-eight; Charlotte Bronte, twenty-five; George Eliot, a mere twenty-two; and John Ruskin, a child of twenty-one.

Even in politics and government it was an era of precocious young men of destiny, among whom Mill enjoyed an admirable position. The immortal Gladstone was two years younger, and the magnificent Disraeli was a scant two years older than Mill. These were his contemporaries; these were his colleagues. The nature of Mill's work sometimes obscures the fact that he was one of the most eminent Victorians. Because of this, it might be interesting to pause to consider what other writers of prominence were doing at this time. For example, in 1843, when Mill's *A System of Logic* was published, Charles Dickens' *Martin Chuzzlewit* joined it in the bookstores, Carlyle published *Past and Present,* Wordsworth was basking in the fresh glory of having been made Poet Laureate, Tennyson's *Poems* and Macaulay's *Lays of Ancient Rome* were attracting much favorable attention, Elizabeth Barrett Browning was working on her *Poems,* and Dumas was creating *The Three Musketeers.* By the time the *Principles of Political Economy* was published, *Dombey and Son, Vanity Fair, Wuthering Heights,* and *Jane Eyre* were best sellers.

I *The Middle Years*

The middle years, 1840-1860, were difficult for Mill in many respects; and insofar as his personal life is concerned, they provide the most unflattering view of the man. The Saint of Rationalism at times revealed himself as something less than beatific. If Mill did not remove himself from his pedestal and reveal his feet of clay, he did at least manage to leave some very muddy tracks. The profound theorist did not always measure up in practice. This failing was particularly evident in his family affairs.

Although gifted with extraordinary powers of intellect that enabled him to come to grips with a vast complex of social problems, Mill floundered about wildly in a morass of personal problems; he struck out blindly and inflicted great pain upon many of those who loved him most. The most charitable conclusion available to his admirers is that although he had learned how to study people, he had not learned how to live among them on intimate terms with any appreciable degree of sympathy and understanding. Ironically, his legalistic mind did not enable him to grasp the admirable art of compromise as an essential aspect of family life.

In his early adult life he had proved that he could be a very genial and engaging young man. He had a pleasant sense of humor and was a skillful conversationalist. Later, much later, he would for the most part regain those social virtues. Now, however, in mid-life, he grew more and more difficult. There is no doubt that his relationship with Mrs. Taylor was the catalytic agent. Moreover, his physical condition was not good. There were extended periods of malaise which probably did little to encourage an even disposition. Added to his indispositions was his growing concern for Harriet Taylor's health—she was virtually a chronic invalid from 1841. When one considers Mill's situation, it is possible to feel genuine pity for him. Nothing, however, can quite remove the shocked dismay at the coldness with which he treated his brothers, sisters and, in particular, his mother, following his marriage.

In 1840, Henry, nineteen years old and the youngest of the boys, died of tuberculosis. He had been a gentle youth, warm and friendly. The boy seems to have been Mill's favorite, and if he had lived, he might have done much to mediate and minimize the subsequent conflicts between Mill and his family. James, another brother, was working for the House, in India, during the period of greatest difficulty in the home; there is little evidence that he had much interest in or sympathy for his more famous brother. Mill, until his marriage, continued to live at home with his brother George, his four sisters, and their mother.[2]

Mrs. Taylor had problems of her own. She had violent quarrels with members of her family, particularly with her sister Caroline and with her brother Thomas. Although her husband was ever kind and understanding, she had trouble with her sons—Herbert, who was devoted to his father, and Algernon. Her daughter, Helen, who was to become Mill's devoted companion in later life, appears to have been a pleasant but placid member of the family. There is some reason to suppose that Harriet's three children, all born within a period of four years,[3] enjoyed a place in their mother's affection so long as they did not interfere with her personal life. There has been some speculation on the significance of this rapidly expanded family and Mrs. Taylor's collateral association with Mill during the same period.

Although Mill's marriage to Harriet Taylor satisfied certain formalities and resolved a number of difficult social problems, it did nothing to remove Mill's estrangement from his family and a number of his friends. In fact, the marriage led to a complete break with his mother, as well as with his brothers and sisters. Not one of them had been invited to the wedding. His brother George did not even know of it until some time later. When he wrote to the newlyweds and expressed his surprise, John and Harriet both rewarded him with arrogant and insulting letters informing him that their marriage was no concern of his. Both of them remained extremely resentful and were quick to take offense at the slightest suggestion of criticism, stated or implied, of their past or present relationship. Their extreme sensitivity caused them to react violently to any word or action that might contain the least tone of disapproval, however unintentional it may have been. Moreover, they had long memories—their resentment was not short lived. This was particularly true in the case of Mill, as he ultimately proved. Once he had become alienated from his family, he rejected all of their subsequent attempts at reconciliation. Not even the death of George or his mother's illness and death[4] could rekindle his affection. A few years before his own death he showed some concern for his sister, Mary, who was then a widow near destitution. He provided her with considerable financial assistance, but he offered her neither love nor comfort.

The letters which he exchanged with his family during this period tell the sad story:[5]

Mary (Mill) Colman to J.S.M., July 18, 1851:

In thinking over the strange change which appears to have taken place in your conduct towards your family . . . I could not help recalling the letters which you sent me . . . which first made me aware that individually I was an object of no interest to you, that you had no affection for me. . . . I ask you how you could act so to Clara who valued you not for your reputation or any other advantages which you could bring to her, but for yourself. . . . How bitterly cruel to refuse to see [Clara] at the India House. . . . Again when Clara determined that your conduct should not make her behave ill to your wife called on her, how did you drive her from your door.

George Grote Mill to H.T.M., May 20, 1851:

Though I have only heard at second hand, of your recent marriage . . . I can only conclude that he [Mill] must have thought me either uninterested in, or undeserving to know. . . . If you feel in me any part of the interest which I feel in you all, you will not leave me in entire darkness. . . . Yours affectionately.

H.T.M. to George Grote Mill, July 5, 1851:

I do not answer your letter because you deserve it—that you certainly do not—but because tho I am quite inexperienced in the best way of receiving or replying to an affront I think that in this as in all things, frankness and plain speaking are the best rule. . . . In my opinion [G.G.M.'s letters] show want of truth modesty and justice to say little of good breeding or good nature which you appear to regard as very unnecessary qualities.

J.S.M. to George Grote Mill, August 4, 1851:

I have long ceased to be surprised at any want of good sense or good manners in what proceeds from you—you appear to be too thoughtless or too ignorant to be capable of either. . . . You profess to have taken great offence because you knew of our intended marriage 'only at second hand.' People generally hear of marriages at 'second hand,' I believe. If you mean that I did not write to you on the subject, I do not know any reason you had to expect that I should.

Clara Esther Mill to J.S.M., March 3, 1852:

I am sorry to hear from my Mother that you considered I had been wanting in civility to Mrs. Mill. . . . I am entirely at a loss to imagine in what my incivility has consisted. . . . You are, to use George's words 'a great and good man' and you see farther than I do. I do not therefore pretend to judge you, I only cannot understand you.

J.S.M. to Mrs. James Mill, March 5, 1852:

I received yesterday two most silly notes from Clara and Harriet filled with vague accusations.

J.S.M. to Mrs. James Mill, June 9, 1854:

. . . I wish again to remind you in case it has not already been done how desirable it is that someone who is fixed in England should be named executor to your will, either instead of me, which I should prefer, or as well as myself.

His mother died less than a week later on June 15, 1854.

It is significant that in Mill's lengthy autobiography one can find scarcely a suggestion of any family affection. Except for admiring references to his father's intellectual stature, his references to his family are curt and cool. He remarks upon the disadvantages which James Mill brought upon himself by marrying and having a large family, "conduct than which nothing could be more opposed, both as a matter of good sense and duty, to the opinions which . . . he strenuously upheld." [6] Beyond this, he offers no acknowledgment of the existence of other members of the family except casual references to the fact that he did have a mother and that there were other children.

The affection which Mill seems to have withheld from his family, at least in later life, was lavished upon his wife. He was an ever-attentive, adoring husband. They worked together with diligence and dedication on a number of ideas and outlines for projected publications, particularly on the plan for his *Thoughts on Parliamentary Reform*. In the interim, Mill published a brief article on women's rights in which he stressed the need for protecting married women and their children from brutal husbands.[7] This was later republished in a somewhat expanded version as a pamphlet. Most of his newspaper articles written during 1850 and 1851 were routine pieces concerning a wide variety of subjects, and all seem to reflect some measure of Harriet's influence on his thoughts and opinions.

By 1853 the quantity of Mill's writing had assumed greater proportions than at any time since he had abandoned the editorship of the *London and Westminster Review*.[8] He published a substantial number of articles for the *Edinburgh Review*, including an elaborate commentary on Grote's *History of Greece* and a penetrating attack on Whewell's *Moral Philosophy*. During this year neither Mill nor Mrs. Mill enjoyed good health. She suffered for some time from a particularly distressing form of rheumatism and neuralgia which severely limited her activities; he was troubled with disturbing chest pains and a chronic cough. Early in 1854 his ailment was diagnosed as tuberculosis.

As the year drew to a close, he began to feel somewhat improved and decided that a tour of Europe and Greece would have a salutory effect on both mind and body. The warmer climate would be a welcome change from the damp cold of an English winter; and, while he did not mention it, a journey would be a relief from Harriet, whose illness had made her even more irritable and tempestuous than usual. He returned six months later.

Mill immediately became engrossed in a number of matters germane to various of his writing projects, especially the *Autobiography* to which he was giving particular attention. At the same time, his responsibilities at India House increased. In 1856 he was appointed Chief of the Office of the Examiner of India Correspondence, a position which he held until his retirement in 1858. Then, after thirty-five years at India House, he was free to devote himself completely to his writing. He had a comfortable though modest pension, a small return from some investments, and the royalties from his published works. Free from any major financial problems and in rare good health, he and Harriet decided on a visit to the Continent. Their plans were completed, and they left England in October. On November 1, 1858, they were in Avignon; on November 3, Harriet died.

She was buried in France, and Mill purchased a small house

near the cemetery. Ten days later he returned to England. The loss of his wife was a shattering experience; he realized that his only escape from his sorrow was his work. He immediately applied himself to his writing with a feverish intensity that would have exhausted a lesser man. *On Liberty, Thoughts on Parliamentary Reform,* and the first two volumes of *Dissertations and Discussions* were published in 1859. The following year he published *Considerations on Representative Government.* For the next two years he worked on *Utilitarianism,* which was finally published in 1863.

II *A System of Logic*

It was about 1837 that Mill discovered Auguste Comte's *Cours de philosophie positive.* He was very favorably impressed by the ideas expressed in this work, and he immediately wrote to Comte. There followed an enthusiastic exchange of correspondence that lasted for several years, though the two men were never to meet each other in person.[9] Their cordial relationship continued until 1845, when the warmth of their friendship was substantially reduced by the publication of Comte's *Système de politique positive.* The association was finally ruptured completely when Mill, possibly at the instigation of Mrs. Taylor, objected to Comte's uncompromising thesis concerning the inferiority of women. The effect of their long exchange of ideas, however, continued to be clearly apparent in Mill's work, particularly in his *A System of Logic.*

Shortly before meeting Harriet Taylor, Mill had become very much interested in the possibility of writing a comprehensive treatise on human knowledge. It seemed quite obvious to him that if philosophical materialism is the basis of social progress and if the essence of philosophy is the discovery of underlying laws and principles of causality, then the key to understanding rests upon a foundation of logic. And so it was that he began writing his *A System of Logic* in 1830, a task that was to occupy much of his time for the next eleven years.[10]

There were to be many interruptions, for this was not his only activity. He resumed his work on the *Logic* in 1837, after a lapse of several years. At this time the first two books, which were concerned with the importance of propositions and with the theoretical basis of the syllogism, had been completed in rough form. It was at this point that he finally came to grips with the Positivism of Comte, which rested upon experiment, observation, and the consequences derived from the laws of phenomenon. This concept dovetailed with many of Mill's own ideas, and provided fresh impetus to his work. Above and beyond this, there was his strong approval of Comte's insistence that the improvement of society was contingent upon the moral and the intellectual advancement of the people. It seems reasonable to assume that an additional stimulus was probably derived from the publication, in 1837, of Whewell's *History of the Inductive Sciences*,[11] a work that contained many ideas which Mill was eager to challenge from Hamilton's *Logic*, published in 1830, and from his *Speculative Philosophy*, which appeared in 1838.[12] Both of Hamilton's works clashed with Mill's views and invited a rebuttal.

Of all the products of Mill's prolific pen, the *Logic* most clearly demonstrates his philosophic acumen and his mastery of the precise explanation essential to effective expository writing. In attempting to teach others to differentiate between what is ephemeral and superficial and what is of lasting weight and worth, he proceeds with inexorable directness in his analysis of inductive proof. His consuming passion for accuracy finds full expression as he sets forth his stern canons of logic and determinedly emphasizes the creative power of the human mind. Indeed, this work deserves a place beside Aristotle's treatise on the same subject.

Mill, in a letter to John Sterling, provides an excellent statement of the essential nature of his logic: "Mine professes to be a logic of experience only, and to throw no further light upon the existence of truth not experimental, than is thrown by showing to what extent reasoning from experience will carry us. Above all, mine is a logic of the indicative mood only—the logic of the imperative, in which the major premise says not is but ought, I do not meddle with." [13] All reasoning, according to his point of view, is essentially a matter of induction. He recognizes the great opportunity for error that is inherent in syllogistic reasoning because its conclusiveness is entirely dependent upon mutual agreement concerning the propositions involved.[14] Such agreement of propositions depends upon the agreement of the concepts or terms which they contain. But these concepts, in turn, must refer to things, and the great need is that they must correctly refer to these things. It is this element of uncertainty that makes the syllogism particularly vulnerable to subtle falsification and to the invalid conclusions which must inevitably follow. Only through the precision of inductive reasoning can this weakness of the deductive process be avoided.

A number of theorists exerted an influence on Mill's inductive orientation and on his dedicated espousal of logical Positivism.[15] It was from Comte, however, that he derived his concept of the Inverse Deductive or Historical Method.[16] The question that Mill continually posed for himself was: How can we get, from the result of a particular observation, a general law that we know to be true? He found the answer in the division of the various elements or factors present in a problem in order to identify the precise nature of that problem. This process, he saw, also revealed the inner relationship of the parts to each other and to the whole, and it involved an examination of the way ideas function within a particular context. A proper basis for judgment rested on delineating and defining the various qualities, causes, effects, motives, and possibilities. This ability to simplify that which is chaotic or confused by separating it into its constituent parts is fundamental in establishing causal relationships. But the application of principle presupposes knowledge. Consequently, there must be a clarification of what is meant by knowledge.

The only source of knowledge—and therefore the only acceptable form of evidence—is experience. Experience contains within itself the essential features of thought which make for explicit logic. The mind must be regarded as being entirely dependent upon the senses for this information. The mind, when engaged in the reasoning process, contributes nothing itself except to relate actual experience to the problem at hand. Insofar as such relationships are concerned, the future must be regarded as a continuation of the past to which it is, for better or for worse, firmly and inseparably linked. Any prediction as to future eventualities must be predicated upon what will happen—not upon one's concept of what should happen. Mill's central thesis is that real value attaches only to objective fact and genuine possibilities; no value should be given to nebulous hypotheses and subjective forms of wishful thinking.

Logic, as the science of the operation of the mind, must concern itself with phenomena appreciable to the senses, and no knowledge is valid except that which is derived through the senses. It is the phenomena thus perceived by the senses that provide experience, the raw material for the thought process. Thinking, in turn, involves memory and association, an inductive process based on experience. Only one assumption is required: What has happened once will happen again under identical conditions. From a specific instance, followed by a series of identical instances, one arrives at a general law. Thus, in induction one moves from the specific to the general, and the conclusion is always greater than the initial observation or premise. The contrary is true of deduction.

According to Mill, the syllogism, foundation of deductive reasoning, was useful only as a device for classification. Deduction is based on a major premise, followed by a minor premise or specific instance, which leads to a logical conclusion. For example:

> *All men are mortal*
> *Socrates is a man*
> *Therefore Socrates is mortal.*

In this categorical syllogism one deduces that everyone in the category of *men* possesses a specific characteristic, that of being *mortal;* if Socrates is a true member of this category, he must possess this distinctive characteristic. But, Mill maintained, mutually exclusive categories must be initially identified through specific experiences and observation. Therefore, the so-called deductive reasoning is really based on induction and exists only as a classification system for applying the truths already established inductively.

Mill also provided a working solution for situations in which the phenomena observed cannot be adequately explained or accounted for on the basis of available evidence. When a general law is not obtainable, because observation and experimentation have not provided sufficient data for analysis and association, one may substitute an Empirical Law, or a law of provisional validity. This is not so good as an established law, but it is better than a mere hypothesis, and it is subject to modification or replacement as knowledge increases.

The *Logic* was completed in 1840, revised the following year, and finally published in 1843. This was Mill's usual procedure; everything that he wrote went through at least one major revision.[17] He was convinced that there was great advantage in this system of double redaction, that it enabled him to combine the freshness and vigor of the initial version with the superior precision and completeness that resulted from revision.

III *Principles of Political Economy*

Mill began writing the *Principles of Political Economy* in the autumn of 1845, and his manuscript was ready for the printer before the end of 1847.[18] As a book of manifest economic speculation, its subject matter was the production, the distribution, and the use of income, wealth, goods, and services. Although it was not Mill's direct purpose to imbue his readers with the idea of absolute probity in a competitive economy, he entered deeply and extensively into the nature of man's desire for wealth, which he considered as the almost universal motivating principle in the economic complex. This book was his second major work, and it represents his most original contribution to economic theory. As such, it also represents the climax of study, of preparation, and of a sustained effort to revitalize this field of study. The book was a purely scientific achievement, and much of what he has to say has become obsolete or seriously eroded by the changing times. Nevertheless, it is still looked upon by many scholars as the most portentous of his works. In any event, Mill did succeed in explaining the essential and abiding character of his Utilitarian ethic, the doctrine of a political economy based on social consciousness and moral principle. The ideas that social solidarity and loyalty are the binding elements of a nation and that it is the duty of the individual to be ready to assume his share of the responsibility is a truism that time has not altered.

This work, which was to become, for a time, the bible of liberalism, reflects the ideas Mill had set forth in many of his early essays on government, especially in the *Essays on Some Unsettled Questions of Political Economy*.[19] Mill tells us that these were originally "written with no immediate purpose of publication; and when, some years later, I offered them to a publisher, he declined them. They were only printed in 1844, after the success of *A System of Logic*." [20] The *Principles of Political Economy,* incidentally, is a substantial volume consisting of five books and a total of seventy-three chapters.

His treatment of his subject was not new, as he acknowledges in the Preface. Rather, his was an attempt to resurvey the field and to adopt political and economic theories to the new ideas and new applications derived from recent extensions of knowledge. Unfortunately, it is not man's destiny to live in strict accordance with social and political theory, however profound and nobly inspired. The human drama, no less than progress—a synonym for perpetual change—requires that the best theories be continuously reviewed, revised, and perhaps abandoned.

Of course, Mill was aware of this, and he was not lacking in farsightedness. Because of this very fact, much of what he had to say has retained its value, and respect for his acumen has increased rather than diminished. What better reason can one find for the repeated surges of interest in his ideas? Equally impressive is the fact that, although certain of his sociopolitical tenets have not survived the vigorous criticism the years have brought, his high sense of responsibility has never been seriously questioned by even his most violent opponents.

"Writers on Political Economy," he reminds his readers, "prefer to teach, or to investigate, the nature of wealth, and the laws of its production and distribution." In so doing, they must never lose sight of the fact that their subject is "inseparably intertwined with many other branches of social philosophy." [21] Consequently, the influence of the progress of society on the production, distribution, and exchange of wealth must be carefully weighed on one hand, and the influence of government on the other. Mill contends that man invariably seeks wealth; that economic theory depends on dynamic relations and must adjust to time and circumstances; that improved economic conditions inevitably result from improved social conditions. This point of view leads him to adopt "the practical maxim, that the business of society can best be performed by private and voluntary agency." [22]

In setting forth fundamental propositions respecting capital and the laws and conditions relating to the production of wealth, he stresses the general characteristics of a progressive state of wealth. These are: first, a tendency toward increased control over the powers of nature; second, increased security; third, increased capacity for cooperation. Insofar as the proper role of government is concerned, he believed that *laissez-faire* should be the general rule, while admitting certain necessary functions of authority. In this respect, he followed the precedent set by Adam Smith and David Ricardo.[23] Government intervention, in broad terms, serves a proper end only when it serves the physical and moral well-being of the people. He was firm in his insistence that government should not interfere with the natural laws that govern our economy, but he further stated: "It is, however, necessary to add, that the intervention of government cannot always practically stop short at the limit which defines the cases intrinsically suitable for it. In the particular circumstances of a given age or nation, there is scarcely anything, really important to the general interest, which it may not be desirable, or even necessary, that the government should take upon itself, not because private individuals cannot effectually perform it, but because they will not . . . the public either being too poor to command the necessary resources, is too little advanced in intelligence to appreciate the ends, or not sufficiently practiced in joint action to be capable of the means." [24] Finally, Mill provides for the circumstances under which exceptions can be made in the application of the various socio-economic principles which he has evolved from the established laws of political economy.

Mill's *Political Economy* sets forth a complicated system in which the individual could seem insignificant, but this would be a gross error. Mill's whole approach is predicated upon a wonderful faith in his fellow man. He says:[25] "Mankind are capable of a far greater amount of public spirit than the present age is accustomed to suppose possible. History bears witness to the success to which large bodies of human beings may be trained to feel the public interest their own."

Although at times Mill's intensity is difficult to bear, the book is a remarkable achievement. He is not only successful in assailing an insecure era, but he remains severely free from the hysterical apathy of the times. Moreover, unlike certain of his reform colleagues, he does not maintain that the situation will be resolved by some vague sort of revolution. He insists that the somber truth is that a number of important advances could be immediately achieved if a reasonable number of reasonable men would lend support to requests for reforms, and if they would demand that all laws be enforced vigorously but fairly.

For this unification of forces, philosopher-statesmen could provide the necessary leadership. Ultimately, this leadership by the intellectual elite must be indissolubly paired with an educated public. This process is concomitant with Mill's democracy. He realized that the advancement of a democratic form of government is contingent upon a corresponding advancement in the education of the general public. Only in this way will the public come to recognize clearly the necessity for surrendering individual liberties in order to secure the general good.

With the *Political Economy* completed and ready for the press, Mill might have relaxed. The profound economic and social crisis of 1846-1848, however, tormented him. In Ireland, where the economy had been in a steady decline, disaster struck with the ruinous potato famine; thousands died of starvation, and millions were driven from their native land by hunger and want.[26] The Emerald Isle was stricken by typhus, dysentery, and blight. Across the Channel in France, the tottering monarchy of Louis Philippe collapsed.

The latter event aroused mixed feelings in Mill. Louis Philippe, who had obtained the throne as a result of the July Revolution in 1830, had shown promise of being a liberal monarch. By 1848, however, a failure of the harvest caused by floods, a drastic reduction in industrial productivity accompanied by widespread general unemployment, and a series of outrageous political scandals brought about complete economic collapse. There were ugly mass demonstrations, in which the disgruntled army participated. Louis Napoleon seized the opportunity to force the King's abdication and to overthrow the monarchy. He then established the Second Republic, with himself as president. To all outward appearances, this was a democratic move; but on December 21, 1851, Louis Napoleon completed his *coup d'état* when a plebiscite sustained his authority and gave him the power to revise the constitution. By late 1852 he succeeded in having himself declared hereditary emperor and thus ushered in the Second Empire; he assumed the throne as Napoleon III.

Mill regarded these events as the end of all hope of freedom in France, and he wrote numerous articles on the subject. He also revised the *Political Economy* in the light of the changes impressed upon him by the circumstances which had given rise to these disturbing conditions. Then he decided that there was much more work to be done, which he was prepared to do.

IV *On Liberty*

By 1859 the impact of the Industrial Revolution had acquired tremendous force. Although there was a decline in the influence of the landed gentry and the aristocracy, the emerging industrial leaders were equally calloused where human values were concerned. There was still a terrible traffic in human misery in England, and among the poor and the underprivileged there was restlessness and ferment. Beneath the clearly apparent oppression of the many by the few, the discerning eye and ear of the social critic could discover the unmistakable signs and sounds of democracy on the rise. Mill amplified the unrest with *On Liberty*, which was to carry its message into the twentieth century.

On Liberty, a tightly written essay, is so closely reasoned that it must be read carefully in order to be fully comprehended. In it Mill methodically explores the loose and mutable boundaries between proper and improper use of power. He sets forth a magnificent defense for the individual's freedom of action and for the guarantee of private rights. Every man, he insists, is entitled to protection against the tyranny of public opinion as well as against governmental oppression. Individual independence is a right that must never be sacrificed to the collective opinion of the majority. Toward this end, the essay, as Mill points out, has as its objective the assertion of "one very simple principle." [27]

That principle is, that the sole end for which mankind are warranted, individually or collectively, in interfering with the liberty of action of any of their number, is self-protection. That the only purpose for which power can be rightfully exercised over any member of a civilized community, against his will, is to prevent harm to others. His own good, either physical or moral, is not a sufficient warrant . . . over himself, over his own body and mind, the individual is sovereign.

Insofar as the domain of individual liberty is concerned, Mill enumerates in great detail the elements of freedom associated with the traditional concept of "life, liberty and pursuit of happiness." These are: freedom of thought and opinion, and the expression, in public or in private, of these thoughts and opinions; freedom of personal conduct, provided that it imposes no harm on others; freedom to choose one's own friends and associates, "for any purpose not involving harm to others." [28] Through freedom of speech and discussion, falsehood will be filtered out and truth will not only survive but will also be strengthened by the impact of opposed opinions.[29] He tells us:

First, the opinion which it is attempted to suppress by authority may possibly be true. Those who desire to suppress it, of course deny its truth; but they are not infallible. They have no authority to decide the question for all mankind, and exclude every other person from the means of judging. To refuse a hearing to an opinion, because they are sure that it is false, is to assume that their certainty is the same thing as absolute certainty. All silencing of discussion is an assumption of infallibility. Its condemnation may be allowed to rest on this common argument, not the worse for being common. . . . [Second] dismissing the supposition that any of the received opinions may be false, let us assume them to be true, and examine into the worth of the manner in which they are likely to be held, when their truth is not freely and openly canvassed. However unwilling a person who has a strong opinion may admit the possibility that his opinion may be false he ought to be moved by the consideration that however true it may be, if it is not fully, frequently and fearlessly discussed, it will be held as dead dogma, not a living truth.[30]

Having established his basic premise and made clear the general orientation of his thoughts on the subject of liberty, Mill proceeds to elaborate on each of his designated freedoms in turn. First, he warns that truth requires all the support it can get because, contrary to the popular myth that it will always triumph over falsehood, it finds its strength and endurance only when tempered in the heat of discussion and debate.

Moreover, truth is rarely, if ever, absolute. It is, rather, the product of reconciled and combined opposites.[31] Second, freedom of action can not be so broad as freedom of opinion because what the individual does must be weighed against the manner in which it is done and the degree to which it involves the actions of others.[32]

Third, the social contract, as it were, guarantees to the individual the right to seek or to avoid association with others, provided that one's conduct does not violate any specific duty or responsibility to the public. Mill insists that "a person's taste is as much his own peculiar concern as his opinion or his purse." [33] Finally, Mill enunciates the two maxims which he believes provide the foundation for the entire essay. These are: "first, that the individual is not accountable to society for his actions, in so far as these concern the interests of no person but himself. . . . Secondly, that for such actions as are prejudicial to the interests of others, the individual is accountable, and may be subjected either to social or to legal punishment." [34]

Throughout this work, Mill draws heavily upon the thoughts of John Locke, particularly from his *Letters on Toleration* and *Two Treatises on Government;* but he funneled Locke's theories through the filter of French pragmatism espoused by Montesquieu and Voltaire, both of whom insisted that, to be of value, political philosophy must have a practical use. These same intermediaries, incidentally, served in a somewhat similar capacity for the fathers of the Constitution of the United States. In the *Liberty,* Mill also concerns himself with ideas very similar to those of David Ricardo, who focused his attention on the wealthy landowners as the source of England's socio-economic problems and who sought to arouse the public against the landed gentry.

This imposing array of political theorists, and the principles which they applied, provided the historic precedent in accordance with which the efficacy of Mill's ideas could be established. Unfortunately, and perhaps inevitably, Mill left unanswered several important questions—just as his predecessors had done. This, of course, exemplifies one of the great dangers of eclecticism—there is always the possibility that one may collect weaknesses as well as strength from antecedent sources.

It is important to bear in mind that in the *Liberty* Mill is concerned not only with the liberty of the individual but also with the essential limitations to be placed upon this liberty in order to protect the interest of the community. To draw the line intelligently between the value of diverse opinion resulting from intellectual individualism and the danger of influence by those who are not intellectually equipped to assume political responsibility, one must sacrifice certain democratic icons. After the most deliberate consideration, Mill concluded that he had resolved this problem by blending three assumptions: First, many, if not most, of the common people can be educated to meet their political responsibilities; second, there will always be a substantial number who are content to be governed by others; third, only those few who are obsessed by a distrust of government will object to the enumeration of powers expressly granted by the people to their government. Moreover, since it is conceded that there will be a definite limit to the valid exercise of power by the government, individualism will be both encouraged and protected. If any real difference is admitted to exist between government *for* the people and government *by* the people, it exists only insofar as the people are incapable of protecting their own collective rights; and governmental control will decrease in direct proportion to the increase in the ability of the people to remove the need for such control. The essential character of this type of governmental power is different from other democratic versions in that the governed will bear their just share of the burden as they prove that they are equal to the task.

In the interest of completeness, reference should be made to Mill's *Thoughts on Parliamentary Reform,* which is an expansion of his ideas in and was probably intended as a supplement to the *Liberty.* Also published in 1859, it had originally appeared as a political pamphlet about five years earlier. It was primarily concerned with election procedures and with insuring adequate representation for minorities. This work contains an enumeration of election procedures, and it introduces Mill's insistence upon "a plurality of votes, to be given, not to property, but to proved superiority of education." [35]

As though to round out the ideas contained in the *Liberty*— perhaps even to suggest a certain measure of personal dissatisfaction with it—Mill published also in the same year the first two volumes of *Dissertations and Discussions*. They comprise an imposing anthology of essays covering a wide variety of topics ranging from foreign relations and the "currency jungle," through "rights and duties of the State respecting Corporation and Church Property," to gentle criticism of Bentham, praise of Coleridge, and a discourse on the theory of poetry. Most of them had previously appeared in the *London and Westminster Review*, the *Monthly Repository*, the *Edinburgh Review*, and *Fraser's Magazine*. Many were printed in their original form; a few were edited and revised to reflect changes in his point of view; but all were roughly classified by Mill as "minor writings."

CHAPTER 3

Politics and Philosophy

I *A Changed Man*

THE year 1860 introduced not only another decade but another John Stuart Mill. Since Harriet's death he had been dividing his time more or less equally between Avignon and his home in England. Where he was depended on his whim and the weather—and, sometimes, on business. Gradually the intense desire for privacy, which he and Harriet had nourished, was dissipated. He and his stepdaughter, Helen Taylor, indulged their interest in travel and visited Austria, Italy, and Greece. His circle of acquaintances widened as he made new friends at home and abroad. He even visited his old friend Gustave d'Eichthal in Paris and then renewed the delightful correspondence with him that had been allowed to lapse. Mill's home, long closed to all but a select few, was opened to the many; and he entertained them with a warmth and conviviality such as he had not demonstrated for a quarter of a century.

It may be that he felt a certain intellectual relief that had heretofore eluded him. His major published works, commencing with *A System of Logic* and terminating with *On Liberty*, may represent the summit of his literary achievement; in any event, he apparently did not feel the usual pressure to express his views in print. This is not to suggest that he permitted himself to fall into an intellectual lethargy. The consolidated force of his accumulated works had provided an ordering of his thoughts, but they had not calmed his interest and curiosity. His success had confirmed his sincere confidence in the ultimate acceptance of his views. Nothing could shake his belief in this eventuality. Insofar as the present was concerned, he was melioristic—neither optimistic nor pessimistic, but confident of increasing improvement. Things would get better.

Not freedom from activity, but freedom to determine his activity, may have been responsible for his new sociability. Whatever the reason, the reserved, almost tactiturn Mill of the 1850's was now a genial and gracious person.

There was still work to be done, of course, as he reviewed his socio-political *Gestalt* and sought to validate his theoretical knowledge on the basis of continuous observation and experience. This was an endless task which he was to pursue to the very close of his life. His pen was never idle for long.

During 1860 and 1861 Mill composed his essay *The Subjection of Women*, which, however, was not published until 1869. In it he treated a subject about which he had long been concerned, even resentful—male chauvinism. Mill, naturally influenced by his wife, had frequently expressed his disapproval that men had dominated women from the beginning of time. Because he recognized the weighty social factors which opposed his pleas for the recognition of women's rights, he felt called upon to protect their interests. Their inferior position was wrong; it was an evil that was a serious obstruction to true democracy. There was no question of women's ability to fulfill the requirements of full citizenship. All they needed was education, and then they would prove themselves the equals of their male subjugators. If the value of a literary work can be measured by the controversy which it stimulates, *The Subjection of Women* must be ranked among Mill's most successful endeavors.

II *Considerations on Representative Government*

Anyone who has read Mill's earlier works, as he remarks in his Preface to *Considerations on Representative Government*, "will probably receive no strong impression of novelty" from this volume. It is largely a summary of views advanced in the earlier works. In writing it, Mill was not so much concerned with the development of the fundamental principles of government as with the application of them. It is, however, a more mature work in which he solidifies his political theories, and it is regarded by many as his most ambitious treatise on politics. Although this seems to be a somewhat exaggerated evaluation, it is not without some justification.

Mill was open-minded, at least in his academic discussions,

not opinionated, and he was in no way disposed to accept consistency of viewpoint as a major virtue. He was given to continuous review and analysis of his ideas in the light of new evidence and fresh insight. His ideas were not stored away in his mind for the sake of preservation. They were forever in a stage of fermentation. There is little cause for surprise, consequently, that he should decide to restate his case with his latest embellishments. In the present instance, he obviously felt a need to undertake a further definition of government, its purpose, and its functions.

It is one thing to defend the purpose of government. In so doing, it is no difficult task to cater to one's fondest hopes and aspirations. It is quite another thing, however, to outline and to describe the many parts of the political mechanism which will insure the successful operation of a government designed to meet specifications drawn from a theoretical blueprint. Although Mill is rigorous in his approach and thorough in his explanation, the full value of *Representative Government* is realized only through its integral relationship with *Utilitarianism* and *On Liberty*. It is in the former that one finds the essential interpretation of *utility* and the fundamental connection between utility and justice that qualify representative government. It is in the latter that Mill's basic concepts of individual liberty and of the limits to the authority of society over the individual are explicitly set forth. Only after these matters have been settled and their significance firmly fixed in one's mind can proper consideration be given to the precise form of government best suited to the needs of the people.

Many questions immediately intrude themselves. One of the first relates to determining the extent to which those who are to be governed shall be permitted to exercise freedom of choice in choosing their form of government. Mill believed that it was incumbent upon those responsible for determining the best form of government to persuade their countrymen that it is the best.[1] Moreover, the mode of persuasion is of the utmost importance, for the political machine does not function as if by magic. It must be operated, and it cannot function when the people remain passive and inactive. Consequently, it is not enough that they be persuaded to accept a particular form of government: "they must be willing and able to do what it requires of them to enable it to fulfill its purposes." [2] The assumption which Mill makes is that intelligent persuasion is a proper form of intellectual enlightenment and thereby equips the public to make a rational choice in the selection of a form of government. To this extent, the people may be said to exercise freedom of choice.

Another facet of the subject suggests itself, however, since the choice of the people must operate within the confines of known governmental institutions. That is to say, there are not an infinite number of government forms from which to select. The fundamental structures are of a limited variety, and while modification of any particular system is possible, it is usually gradual. Even in the case of violent revolution, the overthrown government is replaced by another form which, although different, is *standard*. That is to say, there is no such thing as an instantaneous creation of an entirely new and original form of government. The change is primarily, and in most cases, exclusively, a change in governmental personnel rather than institutions. A monarchy may be replaced by a republic, a republic by a dictatorship, and a dictatorship by a monarchy. Other less common forms of government are possible, but this does not extend the possible choices to any appreciable degree.

In his commentary on the proper functions of government, Mill merely restates the same views he had set forth in his earlier works. Emphasis is placed on the dynamic nature of governmental controls which fluctuate according to the needs of the governed. These, in turn, are determined by the degree to which the state has advanced. The greater the intelligence, enterprise, and courage of the people, the less need there is for government to act to preserve order and insure progress.[3] To this end, "the most important point of excellence which any form of government can possess is to promote the virtue and intelligence of the people themselves." [4] This is the first criterion of good government.

The second criterion of a good government relates to the actual machinery of that government and "the degree in which it is adopted to take advantage of the amount of good qualities which may at any time exist, and make them instrumental to the right purposes." This requires a government that can provide instruction and guidance for its people.

The form of government most likely to satisfy these criteria is one in which every citizen has both a voice and a responsibility. This is possible, however, only in a state which has become sufficiently civilized to make popular government practicable.[5] Consequently, it must follow that the conditions under which representative government is applicable must be delineated. The fundamental conditions which he enumerates are: (1) that the people are willing to receive it; (2) that they are willing and able to preserve it; (3) that they can, and will, fulfill the duties which it imposes on them.[6]

By representative government, Mill means one in which all, or at least many, of the people can exercise control over the government through their elected representatives.[7] The actual administration should rest with specialists and those chosen to serve in an executive capacity, but final control should be exercised by these representatives of the public. It is their right and obligation to watch over the governmental operations; to keep the public informed; to question, expose, and censure all questionable actions; and to condemn and remove any administrator who fails in the proper conduct of his office or who fails in keeping with the will of the people as expressed through their representatives. For it must be remembered that these representatives:

are not a selection of the greatest political minds in the country, from whose opinions little could with certainty be inferred concerning those of the nation, but are, when properly constituted, a fair sample of every grade of intellect among the people which is at all entitled to a voice in public affairs. Their part is to indicate the wants, to be an organ for popular demands, and a place of adverse discussion for all opinions relating to public matters . . . and along with this, to check by criticism, and eventually by withdrawing their support, those high public officers who really conduct the public business. . . .[8]

Obviously, as with every form of government, there are certain dangers to which representative government is liable. These may be grouped under two headings: those which result

from the ignorance and incapacity of the representatives of th
people, and those which result from their "being under the i
fluence of interests not identical with the general welfare (
the community." [9] Although these difficulties pose a constal
threat to the nation, they would be encountered under an
form of government. The defense available to the people
based upon their willingness to exercise their own intelligenc
and control. An informed and politically active citizenry is
country's only protection against incompetence or "sinister in
terests (to employ the useful phrase introduced by Ber
tham)." [10] If democratic government is to survive, its propo
nents must demonstrate, consistently and increasingly, th
ability of the governed to promote good government. They ca
accomplish this objective only if they have a clear concept (
the true meaning of democracy and can avoid the confusio
that results from misinterpretations of the term. Mill takes cal
to remind his readers:

Two very different ideas are usually confounded under the name de
mocracy. The pure idea of democracy, according to its definition,
the government of the whole people by the whole people, equall
represented. Democracy, as commonly conceived and hitherto prac
tised is the government of the whole people by a mere majority (
the people, exclusively represented. The former is synonymous wit
the equality of all citizens; the latter, strongly confounded with it, :
a government of privilege, in favour of the numerical majority, wh
alone possess practically any voice in the State.[11]

The inequities introduced through a government controllec
or excessively influenced, by a dominating class or by a nu
merical majority are the direct result of restricted suffrage an
of weaknesses in the system of proportional representatior
Most of the difficulties the individual may encounter unde
such conditions can be attenuated by extending the franchis
and by improving the mode of voting. It is to these matter
that Mill next addresses himself, with particular attention t
the Hare system of proportional representation.

In 1859, while Mill was putting together his thoughts fo
Representative Government, Thomas Hare published hi
Treatise on the Election of Representatives. Hare's compli
cated system enables the voter to indicate his relative pref

erence for a number of candidates by ranking them on the ballot in order of choice. The predetermined quota of representatives is then elected on the basis of a mathematical formula which weighs the number of votes for each candidate against the frequency with which he is ranked first, second, third, and so on. The object, of course, is to refine the process of selection through a more careful screening of public opinion. Unfortunately, although the plan does succeed in amplifying the voice of the electorate, it proved much too cumbersome to gain wide acceptance. Nevertheless, it remains a popular subject for debate and, occasionally, it is given experimental application, if only in a modified form on a local level.

Although Mill is not particularly successful in his effort to resolve the voting problem, he does illuminate the question. It must be admitted that he fares no worse than others before or after him; and, in most respects, he is far more logical in his treatment of the subject. His moral idealism has proved to be both the inspiration and despair of practical politicians. Having commented on election procedures, he turns his attention to the period of service that should be allotted to a duly elected representative of the people. The duration of the term in office, he says, should not be so long "as to make him forget his responsibility, take his duties easily, conduct them with a view to his own personal advantage, or neglect his constituents, but long enough to enable him to be judged, not by a single act, but by his course of action." [12]

With respect to executive officers, Mill insists that their work is properly classified as skilled employment and they must therefore be selected and appointed to their positions on the basis of their demonstrated qualifications and ability to perform the duties assigned to them. Such offices should never be filled by popular election.[13]

The remaining sections of *Representative Government* are devoted to a discussion of various supplemental aspects of government. Careful attention is given to local representative bodies upon whom the major portion of the public business must devolve if too much centralization of power is to be avoided. The basic decisions on matters which properly fall within the province of the local authorities must rest upon the degree to which they are primarily a local concern, upon the availability of qualified personnel and facilities, and upon the extent to which such responsibility is "instrumental to the nourishment of public spirit and the development of intelligence. . . . To decide this question it is essential to consider what is the comparative position of the central and the local authorities as to capacity for the work, and security against negligence or abuse." [14] In general, the central government should conscientiously avoid the assumption of any responsibilities that the individual or the community can safely assume: "A government which attempts to do everything is aptly compared by M. Charles de Remusat to a schoolmaster who does all the pupils' tasks for them; he may be very popular with the pupils, but he will teach them little." [15] The government should serve its people, but it should also insist that they become dependent upon such services only so long as they are unable to serve themselves independently of the central government.

One of the most interesting chapters of *Representative Government* is concerned with nationality, concerning which Mill says:

A portion of mankind may be said to constitute a Nationality if they are united among themselves by common sympathies. . . . Community of language, and community of religion greatly contribute to it. . . . But the strongest of all is identity of political antecedents. . . . Whatever really tends to the admixture of nationalities, and the blending of their attributes and peculiarities in a common union is a benefit to the human race. [16]

Mill is fully aware of complications which arise from geographical positions, diversity of race, national history and sentiment, the possible subjugation of a smaller nationality by a more numerous nationality, or of an inferior civilization by a superior one. He has confidence, however, that the joining of such groups can be accomplished in a manner calculated to avoid subjugation by the larger or more highly cultivated group. The solution rests upon a genuine humanitarian interest in the improvement of the lesser nationalities, through education and leadership, which will ultimately establish equality of contribution to the common good.

It is difficult to classify the ideal government, as Mill visualized it, in contemporary terms. Many of his liberal viewpoints are enthusiastically endorsed by the ultraconservatives of today; many of his conservative views are today a part of the doctrine of liberalism. Certain of his views can be, and in fact are, quoted with pleasure and satisfaction by every political camp from the extreme left to the far right. Certainly Mill's ideal government is far removed from Plato's utopian republic; nor can Mill write of an ideal state with anything resembling the measured probabilities of Aristotle. Yet, he borrows heavily from both and also from many others who followed them. Nowhere is he more eclectic in his approach than in his *Representative Government*.

Mill accepts Plato's basic concept of a constitutional democracy, and he adds to it much of Locke's carefully constructed system of constitutional checks. He shares not only Aristotle's concern over the potential tyranny of majority rule but also Rousseau's confidence in the belief that a democratic nation does not need to be protected against the will of its own people. He rejects Rousseau's assertion that all men are born equal and that subordination by artificial means is necessary, and he also opposes Rousseau's tight restrictions on the franchise.

The net result is a detailed dissection of the machinery of government required to provide the people of a nation with necessary services and with security. Legal restraints on the people are carefully balanced against the limits set upon the powers of the government.[17] There is to be control through law and regulation, but this is not the same as Aristotle's strange blend of oligarchy and democracy, nor is it Plato's remarkable government of Supreme Council—philosopher—king. It is, rather, a republican form of government in which the people are educated to rule and to be ruled. What is more, it is sufficiently clear in its democratic focus to identify Mill permanently as one of the outstanding champions of liberalism in the nineteenth century.

Throughout the century, the social and political conditions in England improved. The education and the material status of the people were upgraded as passions for liberty were aroused and as the privileges of the chosen few were cut back. An enlightened public—under the leadership of Mill, Gladstone, Lord Palmerston, and other liberal politicians and political philosophers who had achieved positions of influence—sought to free itself from political restrictions. Gradually the political forces changed character and gave greater recognition to the will of the common man. In any review of the period, Mill's *Considerations on Representative Government* stands out as a convenient inventory of much that was sought and of much that was obtained. Its value, in this respect, remains essentially undiminished, for much that Mill had to say remains worthy of thought and quotation today. The frequency with which his words are repeated in the legislative assemblies and international forums of the world testifies to the efficacy of his thoughts and aspirations.

III *Other Works*

There are two additional works which, though presented slightly out of chronological order, fit conveniently into this period. As was so often the case, the thought and writing antedate publication by a considerable period.

Sometime in 1861 Mill read a collection of published lectures of Sir William Hamilton, whose common sense rationalisms had made him one of the most popular philosophers of the time. Mill had shared many of Hamilton's views and had also regarded him as a sophisticated philosopher who could bridge the gap between the intuitionists on the one hand and the experience-association advocates on the other. Consequently, Mill approached the published lectures with an open mind and was terribly disappointed when he discovered that they were full of inconsistencies and contradictions. It seemed to him that, in the light of such evidence, Sir William could scarcely justify himself as a philosopher. He attempted to prove this by publishing a polemic entitled *An Examination of Sir William Hamilton's Philosophy*. In it he once more launches his attack on knowledge by intuition, and he dismantles the *a priori* reasoning of Rationalism.[18] His arguments are essentially a restatement of the views set forth in his *Logic*.

Perhaps this *Examination* stimulated a fresh interest in such matters, for Mill followed his work on Hamilton with a treatise entitled *Auguste Comte and Positivism*. He maintained that it was incumbent upon him to do so because he himself:

had contributed more than anyone else to make his speculations known in England. . . . The better part of his speculations had made great progress . . . under cover of these better parts those of a worse character . . . had also made some way. . . . Those causes not only made it desirable that someone should undertake the task of sifting what is good from what is bad in M. Comte's speculations, but seemed to impose on myself in particular a special obligation to make the attempt.[19]

Mill's major concern is with Comte's *Système de politique positive*, in which the French philosopher attempts to establish regulatory controls over virtually every detail of life. As Mill had already shown in his major works, he recognized the need for government to exercise general supervision over the actions of the individual and over society as a whole, but he emphatically denied that all the minutiae of life either should be or could be amenable to governmental regulation.

Comte, through his "laws of the three states," sought to bring every aspect of life within the realm of government. This view was an extension of the socialism of Saint-Simon, who had exerted a great influence on both Comte and Mill. The former, who has become identified as the "father of sociology," connected the science of society into a religion of Positivism. It was Comte's belief that man passed through three distinct phases or states in his social development. In the first stage he sought and subscribed to a theological explanation of phenomena, attributing everything to the supernatural offices of whatever gods there were. This period was followed by a metaphysical approach in which he satisfied his desire for knowledge by seeking the answers to his questions in the abstract interpretation of natural forces. Finally, he advanced to a positive position in which he acquired exact knowledge from objective examination of his environment and of the forces which exerted an influence upon himself and society. It is from this last phase that the label Positivism was derived.

Comte's treatment of his subject was brilliant and exerted considerable influence upon many of the most sophisticated philosophers. In disagreeing with Comte, Mill reiterated, succinctly but eloquently, the position he had assumed earlier in *On Liberty* and *Considerations on Representative Government*.

CHAPTER 4

Utilitarian Mission

IT has often been noted by even the more casual historians that some ages appear to emphasize the rational approach to life and its problems; others seem to stress the traditional and sentimental approach. The Victorian age combined both influences in the granite-and-talc profile of its social and political philosophers. Much the same may be said of the complex image of the twentieth century. Indeed, this may help to explain why the present age thinks that it is discovering for the first time many of the ideas that were discussed by Mill, Carlyle, Coleridge, and other conspicuously articulate Victorians. As John Maynard Keynes has remarked, "The ideas of economists and political philosophers, both when they are right and when they are wrong, are more powerful than is commonly understood. Indeed the world is ruled by little else." [1] No matter what Mill might have thought of Keynes' own political and economic theories—had he lived to know them—he would have looked with hopeful favor on this particular dictum. Moreover, insofar as the literary critic is concerned, the works of writers such as Mill deserve special consideration, for—as Matthew Arnold insisted—the critic of books should be first and last a critic of society.

Mill was a social critic; he was a reformer. The measure of his influence can be estimated from the fact that for almost half a century he was regarded as an authority on economic and political theory at such seats of learning as Oxford and Cambridge universities. Outside the classic halls of academia, he was the accepted leader of an entire group of economists advocating reform. (In the *Autobiography* Mill calls himself a socialist). He was an intellectual explorer who was forever searching out the underdeveloped areas of the mind. As one of a galaxy of serious writers, the ideological fallout which followed him has an eternal quality. There is a mass of evidence in his many works to establish the truth of this. An excerpt from a letter that he wrote to Auguste Comte reveals the direct line of communication he has with the twentieth century: [2]

Today all the cry is to provide the poor not only with money but, it is only fair to say, whatever is thought beneficial, shorter hours of work, for example, better sanitation, even education, primarily Christian and Protestant, but not excluding a modicum of secular education. That is to say, they are to be governed paternally, a course to which the Court, the nobility and the wealthy are quite agreeable. . . . They entirely forget or rather have never known that well-being cannot be secured by passive qualities alone and that, generally speaking, what is done for people benefits them only when it assists them in what they do for themselves.

Clearly, Mill was a man with a mission and, in the final analysis, it was a Utilitarian mission. Exactly what is implied in this designation is best explained in his book, *Utilitarianism*.

I *Utilitarianism*

During the last year of his married life Mill had started to work on a treatise in which he presented his revised notions on Utilitarianism. Through the years he remained deeply conscious that his whole training had been designed to prepare him for this task. The time had come for him to carry out his appointed assignment, and he approached it with the familiar determination born of his formative years. Now, however, he found that he could not present himself simply as the enlightened proponent of the ideas he had inherited from Jeremy Bentham and James Mill. He could not pretend to sustain a position to which his own reason no longer gave full and complete assent. His concept of Utilitarianism had changed gradually in form and character in response to the development of his own economic and social theories. He could no longer write in the image of his doctrinal ancestors.

Bentham's philosophical doctrine of utility based on the principle of the greatest happiness for the greatest number had long since clashed in Mill's mind with Carlyle's assertion that there was no such thing as a person's right to happiness. Mill's intellect provided an arena for the ideological turmoil which followed. He did not share Carlyle's mystico-political predilection, and he had no desire to become involved in metaphysical fantasies. On the other hand, he was concerned with the ephemeral characteristics of happiness and with questions relating to the quality and quantity of happiness in specific instances. These were the most difficult questions confronting him, and they were, ultimately, unanswerable. But his search for answers continued relentlessly as he sought to overcome his inner dilemma. The end result was a substantial modification of Bentham's tenets of political evolution.

It seemed quite obvious to Mill that the problems of the common man through all history had derived from an overwhelming lack of understanding and sympathy for him by the ruling classes. Through the years, however, serious doubts had been raised in his own mind concerning the question of whether or not there was any meaning left in Utilitarianism as an answer to this problem. He composed a number of essays on the subject which remained unpublished until 1860 when they appeared as a series of articles in *Fraser's Magazine*. These were subsequently published in a single volume under the title *Utilitarianism*,[3] and they provided a summation of his various attempts to bridge the gap between happiness for the individual and Bentham's greatest happiness for the greatest number.

There is no question that Mill was singularly well qualified to write such a book, or that it was destined to become recognized as a classic in its field. Nor is there any doubt that he succeeded in his express intention to provide in this amazingly compressed volume a succinct but inclusive statement of Utilitarian principles. Doubtless some readers, perhaps many readers, will be inclined to argue that this book possesses little elegance or charm. Such a view may be accepted as a justifiable criticism if one wishes to treat style as something extrinsic to the subject. There are other readers, perhaps most readers, however, who will see in the clear progression and organization of ideas a form of literary excellence that can be achieved only when the author of a work writes with great knowledge and conviction.

The first two chapters, entitled "General Remarks" and

"What Utilitarianism Is," serve essentially as an introduction. In these chapters Mill performs the important task of explaining the aims and objectives of the book, and he undertakes to relate his own concept of Utilitarianism to the antecedent concepts of Jeremy Bentham and, coincidentally, James Mill. This task is achieved through a systematic account of the origin and development of various attitudes and arguments relative to his subject. At the same time, his own views are made abundantly clear.

Concerning the nature of Utilitarianism, Mill says: "The creed which accepts as the foundation of morals, Utility, or the Greatest Happiness Principle, holds that actions are right in proportion as they tend to promote happiness, wrong as they tend to produce the reverse of happiness. By happiness is intended pleasure, and the absence of pain; by unhappiness, pain, and the privation of pleasure." Bentham, of course, had propounded the same idea. He believed that the desire for pleasure—freedom from pain—was an essential characteristic of human nature. He also believed that pleasure was an element mensurable in terms of quantity and quality. Pleasure, he would have one believe, is an end in itself and the natural goal of all men.[4]

These views did not dovetail with Mill's interpretation. Mill realized, first of all, that Utility, if it were to serve as the foundation of morality, had to provide the *summum bonum* for mankind. This necessity might, under various circumstances, require a much broader concept of pleasure. It was not enough to think of it as mere freedom from pain or as personal satisfaction in realizing the achievement of one's goal.

Moral consciousness might easily provide a situation in which the deliberate acceptance of pain—unhappiness—was the ultimate good. "It is noble to be capable of resigning entirely one's own portion of happiness, or chances of it; but, after all, this self-sacrifice must be for some end; it is not its own end. . . . would the sacrifice be made if the hero or martyr did not believe that it would earn for others immunity from similar sacrifices?"[5]

Similarly, though Mill gives qualified approval to the greatest happiness for the grestest number principle, he is ever alert to the paradox and inconsistency that may be encountered in applying it to actual practice. Life should have a rational purpose,[6] and the logical and moral justification for the espousal of this principle as a means toward purposeful living can be delineated, but the end product is inevitably the total involvement of society. That is to say, this rational purpose is socially oriented. In this concept one encounters the classic problems of quality and quantity of happiness as a social utility; for, in attempting to measure pleasure within a social unit, one is not dealing with a single effect but with a very complicated assemblage of effects. There are, Mill warns, "certain social utilities which are vastly more important and therefore more absolute and imperative, than others are as a class . . . and which, therefore, ought to be, as well as naturally are, guarded by a sentiment not only different in degree, but also in kind."[7] Add to these conditions the obviously wide range of individual variations, and one might feel that Utilitarianism deserves but short shrift.

But this reaction is true only if one accepts the innate selfishness of man in his search for his own happiness, as Bentham's tenets suggest. Mill circumvents the objections to which Bentham is particularly vulnerable. Mill sees happiness for the individual as something bound to the common good—not as a selfish concern with mere personal pleasure. His confidence in the reliability of the influence of education leads him to the conviction that the education of man's intellect can remove the selfishness that might otherwise interfere with the improvement of human conduct. This is not to say that man is infinitely teachable, but that he can assuredly learn to identify his own happiness with the general good of society as a whole. There is, then, no limit to what might unfold "under an enlightened direction of social and educational influence."[8] Once a basic pattern has been laid down, man's capacity for living with Utilitarian purpose will extend indefinitely, if very gradually. At the very least, man will come to understand that there are all sorts of happiness, and the best of all is that happiness which is derived from the common good.

The moral implications are quite apparent, and Mill, in the third chapter of the book, offers as a sanction of Utilitarian morality "the hope of favour and the fear of displeasure, from our fellow-creatures or from the Ruler of the Universe, along with whatever we may have of sympathy or affection for them, or of love and awe of Him, inclining us to do his will independently of selfish consequences." [9]

There remains, however, the task of assessing the importance of Utilitarianism in terms of its application to the administration of the affairs of society. How may the machinery of government be adjusted to function properly within its own domain and thus serve this enlightened citizenry with justice? Once more one must begin with an examination of Bentham's position. He maintained that the purpose of government is to insure the greatest happiness for the greatest number of the people governed; that each individual is the best judge of his own happiness and can serve his own interest better than government can; that intervention on the part of government in affairs of the individual was coercion and contrary to the fundamental nature of democracy.

Mill could accept the first of these precepts about the purpose of government, but with reservations. The last two about individual rights he rejected as untenable. Government must indeed serve the people; and, in the performance of this service, it should strive to insure the common good without denying individual liberty. The two objectives are not always compatible, however, and practical legislation based upon Utilitarian social thought requires the sophisticated judgment of expert administrators. If one denies man his liberty, one absolves him from responsibility for his actions. Yet, according to Utilitarian theory, he must be a responsible individual. Unfettered individual liberty, on the other hand, can endanger the general good; and liberty for the individual must yield to the security of the common good.

In his treatment of government and the governed, Mill anticipated many of the present-day problems. This is especially true in his discussion of the two most important functions of government—the administration of justice and taxation. The individual is protected by law; society is protected by law. On the surface, such a straightforward analysis appears very simple. It is not. There is always the possibility that an individual may be given certain legal rights which *ought* not belong to him; the law which bestows these rights on him would then be a bad law. What then?

Some maintain that no law, however bad, ought to be disobeyed by an individual citizen. . . . This opinion (which condemns many of the most illustrious benefactors of mankind, and would often protect pernicious institutions against the only weapons which, in the state of things existing at the time, have any chance of succeeding against them) is defended, by those who hold it, on grounds of expediency. . . . Other persons, again, hold the directly contrary opinion, that any law judged to be bad, may blamelessly be disobeyed, even though it be not judged to be unjust, but only inexpedient; while others would confine the license of disobedience to the case of unjust laws; . . . some say that all laws which are inexpedient are unjust. . . . Among these diversities of opinion, it seems to be universally admitted that there may be unjust laws, and that law, consequently, is not the ultimate criterion of justice, but may give to one person benefit, or impose on another an evil, which justice condemns. When, however, a law is thought to be unjust, it seems always to be regarded as being so in the same way in which a breach of law is unjust, namely, by infringing somebody's right; which, as it cannot in this case be a legal right, receives a different appellation, and is called a moral right.[10]

The point that Mill seeks to make is reflected in a story that is told about a student in one of the most famous law schools in the United States. In one of the student's classes, his professor carefully explained the various facets of a particular case and then announced the decision that had been arrived at by the judge. The student, whose inquiring mind would have been much admired by Mill, rose to ask a question of the professor. "Sir," he said, "I recognize the legality of the judge's ruling, but I am not convinced that it was a just decision." To which the professor replied: "Young man, this is a School of Law, and we are concerned with legality. If you want justice, I suggest that you transfer to a School of Theology."

There are, of course, many avenues of approach to the problem of administering justice. Of all the examples that might be drawn from the *Utilitarianism,* however, the one which serves best to illustrate Mill's discernment, as well as the contemporary value of his argument, concerns taxation. Government must be financed; a major source of support is the income provided from taxation. The eternal question is: How much should be paid, and by whom?

Justice dictates what they [tax experts] term graduated taxation; taking a high percentage from those who have more to spare. In point of natural justice a strong case might be made for disregarding means altogether, and taking the same absolute sum (whenever it could be got) from everyone . . . all pay the same sum for the same privileges. . . . Since the protection (it might be said) of law and government is afforded to, and is equally required by all, there is no injustice in making all buy it at the same price. It is reckoned justice, not injustice, that a dealer should charge to all customers the same price for the same article, not a price varying according to their means of payment. . . . People feel obliged to argue that the State does more for the rich than for the poor, as a justification for its taking more from them: though that is in reality not true, for the rich would be far better able to protect themselves. . . .[11]

We see in this passage both the strength and the weakness of Mill's reasoning. Although he takes giant strides in moving from the general theory of Utilitarianism to specific application in practical affairs, his answers are frequently qualified by alternative possibilities. Not infrequently, the alternatives have much more to recommend them than Mill, or Bentham, would prefer. Moreover, this is true in large measure of the entire book. And it is inevitable that it should be. Not only do many of the questions raised defy solution, but Mill—in spite of his great struggle to be objective—labors under a heavy burden. First of all, he is eclectic in his approach. Most of the principles he discusses were well laid out by others before him, particularly by his father and Jeremy Bentham. And in this heritage we find his problem compounded: He could not overcome completely the subjective influence of his respect and affection for James Mill or the reverence and loyalty which he held for Bentham.

Such limitations notwithstanding, *Utilitarianism* is provocative and contains much to recommend it for study. There are many things to be learned from it that will provide valuable insight into twentieth-century social and economic problems. Moreover, it serves to clarify the picture of John Stuart Mill and makes the popular habit of crudely classifying him as a Utopian socialist or any other variety of radical exceedingly difficult to adopt. Mill requires more than a convenient label.

Much that might, on the surface, seem to qualify him as a radical might, after careful thought, place him firmly on the side of present-day conservatism. The picture becomes more distinct when Mill moves from the quiet of his study and carries his mission to the public platform and to Parliament.

Many of Mill's contemporaries must have reflected from time to time on the inevitability of his ultimate involvement in the political wars on a more personal basis. Generalship has to be tested in action. His intellectual aggressiveness and his enthusiasm for debate presaged such an eventuality. He had already demonstrated his willingness and his ability to engage opponents in argument, for he had on numerous occasions successfully defended his ideas against the masterful attack of some of the greatest minds of the age. It was now time for him to accept the challenge offered by the House of Parliament to test his forensic skill in less sophisticated but in equally strenuous legislative debate—an important part of his Utilitarian mission.

Before reviewing his political career, however, there are two events that deserve special consideration, not only because of their individual merit but also because of the insight they provide into Mill's thoughts and attitudes at the dawn of his parliamentary adventure. The first of these, his public tribute to William Lloyd Garrison, took place immediately prior to his election; the second, his election to the position of Rector of Saint Andrews University, occurred immediately after his successful campaign for public office. The ideas and opinions, both stated and implied, which are contained in the speeches he delivered on these occasions set the tone for much that was to be enunciated in his parliamentary addresses.

II *Tribute to William Lloyd Garrison*

The *Considerations on Representative Government* had concentrated Mill's attention on the United States. America's adventure in democratic republicanism had long been a source of particular interest to him because he could view it as a testing ground for so many of his favorite political theories. His constant observation had enabled him to follow the slavery versus abolition controversy as it developed; and when civil conflict erupted in 1861 he promptly established himself as an advocate for the Union. It seemed abundantly clear to him that the issues were clearly and distinctly drawn. The Confederacy was engaged in a struggle to maintain slavery and a backward agricultural environment in order for a southern aristocracy to retain its class privileges. If this attempt to destroy fundamental human rights and to warp the very structure of the magnificent Constitution of the United States of America were successful, it would be a shattering "victory for the powers of evil." [12]

In January, 1862, Mill published in *Fraser's Magazine* the article "The Contest in America." He continued his protest, and aroused some support among the Liberals for his demand that England stand firmly behind the government of the United States. In fact, he advocated that his country give serious thought to entering the war on the side of the North. In general, however, British sympathy remained with the South because of the belief that the war was actually a struggle for independence; others were anti-United States because of bitter memories of the American Revolution and of the War of 1812. The Trent Affair had done nothing to improve this bias. In November, 1861, a United States warship had stopped the British vessel *Trent,* and removed James M. Mason and John Slidell, two representatives of the Confederate States, who were on a diplomatic mission to England. The commander of the American ship demonstrated an appalling ignorance of international maritime law and nearly precipitated another war with England. Fortunately, Lincoln and Secretary of State Seward were able to placate the London Foreign Office by releasing the prisoners with an apology for the incident.

In Mill's estimate, one of the truly great heroes and spokesmen for the Abolitionist movement was William Lloyd Garrison. A violent agitator, Garrison had formed the New England Society in 1832, an organization later to become the American Anti-Slavery Society. He was also editor of the *Liberator*, a paper devoted to the cause of the Abolitionists. In October, 1835, the office of the paper was mobbed, and Garrison was dragged through the streets with a rope around his neck. He was imprisoned in Baltimore for libel because of his speeches and articles about the slavery question; and Georgia at one time offered a $5,000 reward for his conviction on similar charges. An arrogant, vindictive, and bitter man, he antagonized many sincere Abolitionists by his extravagant demands. At one time he even went so far as to advocate that the North secede from the Union. He survived numerous acts of abuse and continued his relentless attacks on slavery and the South.

When Garrison visited England in 1864,[13] a reception was held for him at Saint James Hall.[14] The London *Times* reported that the hall was thronged, with three hundred people seated at the dining tables on the main floor, a privilege for which each had paid ten shillings. The galleries were packed. John Bright,[15] whose fame as an orator and statesman was well established on both sides of the Atlantic, presided at the speakers' table. Among the guests were such notables as Herbert Spencer, T. H. Huxley, and John Stuart Mill, who delivered a eulogy on the "courageous and singleminded apostle" of human rights.[16]

Mill, in lauding the honored guest, spoke with grace and simple elegance as he pointed with philosophical thoughtfulness to the moral of Garrison's experiences.[17] Two lessons, in particular, were recommended to the attention of his listeners. The first is to "aim at something great; aim at things that are difficult." The second is, "if you aim at something noble and succeed in it, you will generally find that you have not succeeded in that alone." He assured those present that America and all of mankind would be forever indebted to Garrison for having taught these lessons through his own dedication and suffering.

The London *Times,* in the same report mentioned earlier, while praising both Mill and Garrison, commented somewhat cynically, that Mill: "exhorts young politicians to aim high and not to fear the reproof of visionary projects. The advice is good, if taken subject to proper qualifications, but so would be the opposite advice not to sacrifice present duties to passionate yearnings for the redemption of mankind."

III   *Rector of Saint Andrews University*

Shortly after Mill's election to the House of Commons, he won another honor which must have been a source of considerable pleasure and personal satisfaction: He was chosen to be Rector of Saint Andrews University.[18] The honor carried with it the responsibility of an inaugural address. According to custom, this should have been delivered immediately, but the opening of the 1866 session of Parliament required Mill's presence in the House, and so the ceremonies were postponed.

Finally, on February 1, 1867, he arrived at the university for the official installation, which took place before an unusually large audience. It was a dramatic scene, with the students and faculty in full academic regalia. The proceedings were opened with a prayer in Latin. Mill was then invested with his new robe of office and awarded the degree of Doctor of Laws. It is interesting to speculate on his thoughts at that moment, for the scholar who had never set foot inside the halls of learning as a student was now Dr. John Stuart Mill. It is also interesting to speculate on the reactions of James Mill and Jeremy Bentham, had they lived to be present.

Although his inaugural address is not exceedingly fertile in sonorous and imaginative phrases, this oration possesses an eloquent rhetorical quality. It is a fine speech, well organized, carefully worded, and with skillful use of a wide variety of grammatical structures. In many respects, it is his finest speech. The London *Times* carried the following item: "Today Mr. John Stuart Mill was installed into office as rector of the University of Saint Andrews . . . the Vice-Chancellor presented him with the degree of Doctor of Laws. Mr. Mill then delivered his address on the subject of a University education, which was listened to with sustained attention and cordially applauded. It occupied about two hours in delivery." The *Saturday Review*[19] remarked that "few things have lately appeared more worth reading." The *Edinburgh Review* added that his words "have been echoed far and wide beyond the halls in which they were uttered." [20] And the *Dublin Review* asserted that "the great body of Mr. Mill's remarks are worthy of the gravest and most respectful consideration." [21]

Actually, the speech had had a sort of literary prologue. Several years prior Mill had prepared a speech about secular education which was never delivered; it was eventually published as an appendix to his *Autobiography*.[22] In this earlier speech, which might better be called an essay, Mill opposed unreservedly the domination of education by the Church of England. The basis of his opposition was that the catechism and liturgy were taught to all students in all schools except in the few that were privately owned. Such blatant religious indoctrination, he insisted, denied the fundamental right of each individual to be the proper guardian of his own spiritual welfare. Any invasion of this right by an attempt on the part of one person to decide the question of religion for another was a completely unwarranted assumption of infallibility. This Mill found intolerable.

The substance of this speech, which is in essence a précis of his *Three Essays on Religion* (1874), is retained in the "inaugural address." In this Mill's central theme is that mental cultivation should open the mind to all truth. His extended development of this theme, which provides a summary of his total concept of university education, is a stimulating and thought-provoking commentary on education in general.

His conception of the function of education is sound. He offers a provocative and inviting approach to a broad, liberal arts education in the classical tradition. Yet, while his initial preoccupation with rhetoric, literature, philosophy, and the fine arts is impressive, one soon perceives that Mill also recognizes the importance of the new scientific studies, which he fits skillfully and comfortably into his overall program of learning.

The enlargement of his subject is neatly narrowed to an effective focus when he warns that education must not be confined to the learning of subjects of direct and immediate usefulness, but should extend to the encouragement of general cultural growth and broad intellectual attainments. He recognizes the danger that lies in dull uniformity and in routine teaching, and he cautions against failure in the search for ways by which outstanding ability can be properly identified and developed most effectively.

When Mill reaches this point, however, another danger supervenes. He reveals that he has no clear concept of the limits of a university curriculum. His naïveté is understandable, for his own training prevented him from developing an adequate awareness of the practical problems involved in providing mass education. He does not seem to realize that a university cannot be conducted exclusively in the interest of genius, but must strive to meet the demands and to satisfy the needs of the vast multitude of average students.

As he seeks to map out the demands for intelligent and responsible citizenship, he effectively traces the pathway from general knowledge through character development to the practical demands of life. It is an interesting intellectual journey in which two milestones are encountered that can serve to guide men of all generations. The first of these is Mill's insistence that government should be the concern of all. There are those, he reminds his audience, who "will warn you against Political Economy. It is unfeeling, they will tell you. It recognizes unpleasant facts. For my part, the most unfeeling thing I know of is the law of gravity; it breaks the neck of the best and most amiable person without a scruple, if he forgets for a single moment to heed it." [23]

The second is an admonition to all who strive for knowledge: "Let us understand, then, that it should be our aim in learning, not merely to know the one thing which is to be our principal occupation, as well as it can be known, but to do this and also to know something of all the great subjects of human interest: taking care to know that something accurately: marking well the dividing line between what we know accurately and what we do not:" [24]

The great educational experiment had come full cycle. James Mill and Jeremy Bentham, had they lived, might not have been entirely satisfied with the results of their labors. Still, though their fondest hopes may not have been fulfilled, their protégé had completed what they had started. Here, at long last, was the final educational balance sheet; and it left no doubt that the credit side of the ledger had reached imposing proportions.

CHAPTER 5

Member of the House

IN the General Election of 1851 Mill had been offered a chance to stand for Westminster. At the time he apparently had had little interest in the opportunity to embark upon a political career, but his reasons are not clearly defined in the little he had to say on the subject. It seems probable that his recent marriage, his position at India House, his approaching retirement, his poor health, and an imposing prospectus of writing projects contributed much to this lack of interest.

In 1864, however, when he was once again approached on the subject, the situation had changed completely. Appointed Chief of the Office of the Examiner of India Correspondence in 1856, he retired three years later—the same year that Harriet Taylor Mill died in France. Moreover, with the publication of *Utilitarianism,* virtually all of his planned major works had been completed. There was, in short, no great conflict of interests, and few demands were being made upon his time. Consequently, he was favorably disposed toward a change of activity. The promise of new fields to conquer—to say nothing of the acclaim and recognition from which this promise stemmed—presented a challenge that he could scarcely ignore. Mill was modest concerning his abilities and his achievements, but he enjoyed his fame. And why not? Even the philosophers who write most eloquently on the virtue of modesty make sure that their names are displayed in appropriate-sized type on the title pages of their published works.

From 1861 to 1864 Lord Derby and the great Disraeli held the Conservative banner on high and defended the legislative barricades against the middle-class radicals led by John Bright. Although the Whigs were in power, thanks to a feeble majority, the added weight of John Stuart Mill could do much to advance the cause of Liberalism. If there was ever an opportune moment for him to make his grand entrance onto the parliamentary scene, this was it. In a sense, he had been sitting at the center of the whirling sphere of ideas; he was now going to venture to the outer edges, where the momentum was the greatest and the collision of ideas most resounding.

Long before George Bernard Shaw was moved to remark that "those who can, do; those who cannot, teach," the political philosophers had acquired similar depreciatory associations. Their theories have always cut with a dull edge until tempered in the heat of parliamentary debate. It was inevitable that Mill, because of the celebrity of his attainments, would ultimately be called upon to establish by practical example the true measure of his critical sagacity and the principle of the charismatic leadership which he espoused.

Sympathy with the poor and the oppressed had grown rapidly into a firm dedication to the cause of freedom and justice. Crises were frequent in the nineteenth century, when the economic and political issues involved in the ownership of land, in the condition of tenancy, and in the rights of the individual to the profit of his labor became acute. Mill's academic demands for changes in economic and political theory drew him directly into the conflicts of his generation. As he observed in his preliminary remarks to *Principles of Political Economy,* systematic inquiry is often the tardy product of a long course of efforts to achieve practical results. Always ready to challenge any social or political theory that could not be defended in the forum of objective reason, Mill was equally ready to extend this challenge to the defense of his theories in the forum of practical politics.

His entry into the political arena was not at all what one might expect from a candidate for a seat in Parliament. When he accepted the nomination from Westminster, he refused to spend any money on the traditional political fanfare. Although he believed that it was his duty to serve the public, he also believed that it was the public's duty to elect him without requiring that he pay for the privilege of serving.[1] Moreover, he was not interested in the traditional task of conciliating and representing any special party or interest group. He believed that election to public office called for trust in his ability, not in his role as spokesman for a group; and he had no intention of placing himself in a position where he could be called upon to surrender his convictions on questions of principle in political or economic issues. He was convinced that his sole responsibility was to his own conscience. Consequently, he took no personal part in the campaign until about a week preceding the day of nomination. Then he relented enough to attend a few public meetings in order that he might state his principles and provide the voters with an opportunity to have any questions answered.[2] His answers to all such questions were unusually direct and succinct.

On one occasion, in keeping with his habit of giving fullest publicity to even his most unpopular views and opinions, Mill was particularly successful at surprising his audience with his outspoken honesty. While on the platform answering questions during one of his few campaign appearances, he was challenged by a supporter of his opponent who asked him if it were true that in an article on parliamentary reform, which Mill had written in 1859, he had referred to the members of this constituency as liars. Mill, quite unruffled by the question, replied that it was common knowledge that English workingmen are generally liars. He observed further that the members of this particular audience were, for the most part, workingmen; the conclusion was thus quite obvious.[3] The listeners were indeed amazed, but delighted with such a direct and forthright answer. That he made no pretense of discarding or shading his opinions to court favor was typical of his brusque honesty.

There was one point in particular which he insisted be quite clear in the minds of all who would vote for him. In whatever concerned the state, he maintained, he would use only his own discretion, even at the risk of offending the House of Commons and all who had sent him there—a rather astonishing plank in any political platform.

In spite of his unorthodox method of campaigning, Mill was elected to the House of Commons from Westminster in 1865, and he served there from February, 1866 until July, 1868. When he arrived in the House of Commons, it was almost as though he were a political Cincinnatus[4] summoned from his bower of theoretical speculation to do battle with his opponents in the parliamentary arena. And Mill quickly discovered that his formal idealistic position had to be modified in practice if he were to win support for his views. In the pursuit of his aims he showed little regard, however, for careerist ambition, and he remained single-minded in his purpose. He was determined to remain untouched by *"la politique, la grande suborneuse,"* and he had the moral fortitude to sustain his determination.

At this period in England's history, "representation of the people" was synonymous with "parliamentary reform." As such, it had a history that could be traced back directly to 1769. In those early years agitation for more equitable franchise and, consequently, for more equitable representation in Parliament was relatively mild. The stage was set, however, for the more rigorous demands which would inevitably follow.

Constitutional reform was debated in Parliament as early as 1770, as some sought to reduce the power of the king and to make the House of Commons more representative of the will of the people. From 1776 on, acts designed to improve representation were repeatedly introduced. They were defeated with equal regularity. Finally, in 1782, the Place Acts were passed. Passage was, at best, a minor achievement, but it did provide the public with somewhat greater voice in the popular elections.

Reform made its first major stride in 1831, when Lord John Russell introduced a very liberal measure. The collapse of his government which followed was unfortunate, but the agitation which it provoked resulted in the passage of a similar but more moderate reform bill the following year.[5] A more equitable system of representation was established and the franchise extended accordingly. This progress, while not entirely satisfactory to the more determined Liberals, served to placate the reformers.

From Mill's point of view, his era was above all a time for reform, and he had sought to revive the spirit of the reform movement when he published his *Thoughts on Parliamentary Reform* in 1859. In it he presented essentially the same arguments which he subsequently propounded in his speeches before the House. He demanded, among other things, universal suffrage, plurality voting, and greater representation of minorities.[6]

The first of his speeches on the topic of suffrage was presented at the second reading of Gladstone's bill to "extend the right of voting at elections of members of Parliament in England and Wales." On March 12, 1866, this measure had been introduced for its first reading, the initial step in presenting any bill for consideration by the House. At the second reading, a bill is normally discussed from the point of view of its general principles, and it can be accepted or rejected at this time.

In keeping with parliamentary practice regarding important cases, the Reform Bill was turned over to a Committee of the Whole House, which was the House sitting under the Chairman of the Committee. Inasmuch as there was no limit on debate, the discussion of the Reform Bill was frequently interrupted in order that other matters might be considered. Consequently, the debate extended over a period of four months. This is one of the ways in which a bill could be delayed indefinitely, and it is also the reason Mill found himself delivering speeches on aspects of the bill which were never brought to a vote. This, in turn, poses a problem when attempting to evaluate the influence he exerted.

When Mill obtained the floor to present his initial address, he had been preceded by an aggressive and talkative collection of orators for the opposition whose speeches had been marked by extravagant phrases that made no substantial contribution to the debate. Mill focused attention not on "the vague abstraction, the good of the country, but the actual, positive well-being of the living human creatures who compose the population." The clerk who recorded the speech noted that Mill "spoke amid continued interruptions and cries for a division. . . . These manifestations of impatience continued to the end of the debate." [7] Roebuck called this maiden speech "an epoch in Parliamentary oratory . . . the outpouring of a great honest yet modest mind; the vigorous expression of well considered and accurate thought." [8]

Mill's skill in the logical marshaling of ideas is clearly demonstrated as he sets forth a method of appraising the value of any measure: "Measures may be recommended by their principles, or by their practical consequences; and if they have either of these recommendations they usually have both." He then applies this principle to the issue before the House—the right of the workingman to express his will and to obtain adequate representation through an extension of the franchise: "As far as regards the principle of this measure there is but little to disagree about . . . the House is not divided on any question of principle here."

Mill then turns his attention to the question of practicality: "It is required by class theory, which we all know is the Conservative [the opposition] view of the Constitution—a favorite doctrine of the Conservatives [that] individuals cannot complain of not being represented as long as the class they belong to is represented. But if any class is unrepresented, or has not its proper share of representation, relatively to others, that is a grievance." Consequently, it follows that: "Now, all that need be asked at present is that this theory be applied to practice . . . there is a class which has not yet had the benefit of the theory [a] class more numerous than all others. . . . It is weak . . . therefore needs the representation the more. [Moreover] it is daily growing stronger and more capable of making its demands good."

In addition to the element of justice, involved in this issue, there are the more obvious advantages that will accrue to the government by virtue of equitable representation for this class: "Every class knows some things not so well known to others. . . . Every class has interests which are more or less special to itself [consequently, representatives of the workingman would provide a valuable source of information, badly needed in the House, because not] a member of the House . . . thoroughly knows the workingmen's views on trade unions or strikes . . . and can present it satisfactorily." His conclusion follows in natural order, as he asks that "[the workingmen receive] sufficient representation to ensure their opinions being fairly placed before the House [so that problems peculiar to their position may be] met with real argument [and arguments of the opposition may be] addressed to their own reason. . . . Let workingmen have equal opportunity to plead their own cause. . . . Let them feel that the contest is one of reason and not power."

Two years later, Lord Dufferin, who had held ministerial appointments in Palmerston's government and under Gladstone, in explaining that the opposition, while accepting Mill's general maxims, felt compelled to dissent from his special recommendations on reform measures, said: "There is no one . . . who has a more profound respect for the intellectual power and pure integrity of purpose displayed in every word that has ever been said or written by one of the greatest thinkers of our time." [9]

When on May 31, 1866, Mill spoke on the subject again, he enjoyed a more responsive audience.[10] This time he attempted a further development of the ideas previously presented. Again, on July 17, 1866, he sought to defend the Reform Bill, and rose to move for the "Return to the number of Freeholders, Householders, and others in England and Wales who, fulfilling the conditions of property or rental prescribed by Law as qualification for the Electoral Franchise, are excluded from the Franchise by reason of their sex." The motion for amendment was voted on and agreed to by the House following his speech. The entire bill then went down to defeat when it was withdrawn by Gladstone two days later.[11]

Although the Reform Bill received a major share of Mill's attention in the House of Commons, he was not without other causes with which to concern himself. Among other things, he urged the government to reduce the national debt and taxes. The question arose in connection with the Malt Tax,[12] then under consideration by Parliament. Some years earlier Mill had published an article on this subject in the *Morning Chronicle*.[13] He had also been invited to appear before a Select Committee of the House to answer questions on taxation prior to his election.[14] Consequently, he was eminently qualified to speak with authority. He supported this particular tax bill on these grounds: First, it was the responsibility of this generation to leave the state in as good a financial condition as it had found it, if not in a better one and not to pass its burden on to posterity; second, it was a just tax because it would be placed on a luxury enjoyed primarily by those who were confirmed beer drinkers.

He rallied to the support of Erin when the Irish Land Bill was submitted for a second reading.[15] Together with Bright and other Liberals, he warned the government that large and bold measures alone could cure Ireland. It was one of his most carefully prepared speeches,[16] and in it he demonstrates his great facility for bringing both social and moral phenomena within the scope of his economic inquiry. The speech also illustrates the functional simplicity of his logic and the directness of his conclusions. First, he asks what is desired in Ireland; second, he offers a plan and shows why it is the only solution; third, he shows how the plan will operate in practice. These steps are then developed:

1. What does the government seek to achieve? Reform of the agrarian economy in Ireland in order to improve agriculture and encourage greater satisfaction among the farmers.

2. How may this be done? There are only two possible solutions: Get rid of the present crop of farmers and replace them with men who are more easily contented, or find means of satisfying those who presently inhabit the land. The first possibility must be rejected for it is impossible to evict a nation. Thus there is but one solution available.

3. What are the needs which must be met? The farmers must be given the encouraging influence of ownership, a real interest in improving the farms, a feeling of security, and an opportunity to enjoy the fruits of their labors. His proposal, Mill says, will do all these things.

4. How will the plan work? The tenant will be awarded compensation by an impartial tribunal for whatever increased value he has given the land. The bill appoints a tribunal. Whenever parties do not agree the case will be adjudged by authorities who possess the confidence of both landlords and tenants. Valuers will be appointed by the government's Board of Works. Provisions will be made for handling appeals.

Another subject upon which Mill had much to say during this session was the outbreak in Jamaica. His first speech, delivered on July 19, 1866, was but a preface to the major address which followed on July 31. In his *Autobiography* Mill refers to the latter as the address which he would probably select as the best of his speeches in Parliament.[17] He had taken pains to investigate the situation in detail, and he presented a closely reasoned argument for the punishment of officials who had mistreated the colonials.

The disturbances in Jamaica resulted from the flogging of women, the massacre of unarmed peasants, promiscuous hanging, and the complete subordination of civil right to military might under Governor Eyre. The situation was the epitome of all that Mill regarded as evil in government. It was natural that he should react violently.[18] He and Herbert Spencer formed a committee to promote the prosecution of Eyre. During the entire episode feelings ran high, for there were many who viewed Eyre's actions as a simple expression of the imperial prerogative to subdue the colonies by any means. After a prolonged debate, the case was eventually brought to trial, and Eyre was acquitted. Once again Mill had been eloquent in support of a lost cause.

During the last weeks of the 1866 session of Parliament, Mill limited himself to two discourses: The first was on the freedom of speech and public discussion as questioned in connection with a protest meeting of the London Reform League held at Hyde Park;[19] the second speech dealt with extradition treaties, and subsequently evolved into an article on treaty obligations published in the *Fortnightly Review*.[20]

Disraeli and the Conservatives returned to the parliamentary session of 1867 with another Reform Bill, and Mill returned with a continuation of the basic arguments he had set forth in the debate of the previous session. The "conservative" Reform Bill, which was to prove successful, was actually more liberal than its predecessor in that it extended the vote among the urban working class and modified the property qualification.

It was the property qualification clause of the bill that occupied Mill's attention when he spoke on May 9, 1867. He set out to clarify the conditions under which a man might satisfy the requirement that he own or rent a house, or part of a house, continuously for one year before being allowed to vote. On May 17 he expanded his comments on occupational franchise. Three days later he rose again to move for the admission of women to the electoral franchise, and he vigorously attacked the practice of classifying women with children, fools, and lunatics by depriving them of the right to vote. Subsequently he presented his argument in moving for the adoption of an amendment based on the Hare system of representation.²¹ The amendment was later withdrawn and never came to a vote.

On June 27, he directed his rhetorical fire against political campaigning and the financial investment which a candidate had to make in seeking public office. Then, on July 5, he delivered his final message on the Reform Bill; in it he deliberated upon a subject which had provoked violent disagreement in the House: representation for minority groups. His recommendations were conservative, his presentation languid, his listeners indifferent. The debate had already extended over three months, and the orators were weary. Disraeli's Reform Act of 1867 was passed, and Gladstone, Bright, and Mill could feel confident that their powerful influence was largely responsible for its passage.

During this session Mill also spoke on the Metropolitan Poor Bill and on the legality of Sunday lectures. The former was a good speech, but it accomplished nothing; the latter was little more than an academic exercise delivered in a jocular vein. He made an unusually brief and placid comment on martial law, and then he retired to the sidelines for the remainder of the session.

On March 6, 1868, Mill brought the American Civil War into the House of Commons. As soon as the session opened, he spoke in the House in support of a bill which proposed that the United States be reimbursed for the damage suffered from the action of the *C.S.S. Alabama,* a vessel constructed in England for the Confederacy. Supporters of the measure suggested that John Bright be appointed a special negotiator to undertake a mutually satisfactory settlement. The plan was a wise one, for Bright was already well-known in the United States for his Union sympathy.

Mill, who had been a Union sympathizer from the beginning and a lifetime opponent of slavery, favored liberal concessions. He was opposed by some members of the House who felt that it might be an opportune time for England to take a stand against her former colony. Moreover, the United States was exhausted from the long war, and there were those who could see no point in giving money to a country that was not strong enough to enforce its demands. Mill assailed both the morality and the legality of such views. His words were well received, and England eventually paid $15,500,000 damages to the United States.

In this final session, Mill's greatest debate efforts were given to the question of corrupt practices among candidates for public office. He proposed that there should be local inquiries by persons of competent legal qualifications after parliamentary elections.[22] Unfortunately, he was unable to overcome the complacency born of traditionalism and convention in politics, and he was told that his scheme was so chimerical that the time of the House should not be wasted by answering it.

In a sequel to this speech, presented on July 22, he extended his criticism to the practice of employing paid canvassers or agents other than those appointed by law to support a candidate for public office in his attempt to obtain votes. He maintained that this practice was illegal and advocated that measures be taken to prevent it. Mill's protests, although eloquently presented, were futile. The opposition, instead of replying to his arguments, concentrated on parliamentary intricacies and hairsplitting. His opponents succeeded in bringing about a division of the House, and his proposal was defeated.

The *Westminster Review* gave considerable attention to an address on capital punishment[23] presented by Mill during this session. It reported that the debate excited more than the usual amount of interest because of Mill's participation, and it went on to offer what could well serve as a eulogy by the opposition on the close of his parliamentary career:

Though not belonging to the considerable class who believe his arguments conclusive, we cannot but regard his speech as an important step toward the satisfactory settlement of the question. The next best thing to having Mr. Mill for a friend is to have him for an opponent. You may not learn from him the full strength of your own case, but you at least have all the difficulties to be encountered arranged in the clearest and most forcible manner, without taint from sophism or exaggeration.

The record of John Stuart Mill, M. P.—for it proved to be his first and only term as a member of the House of Commons —shows that he consistently propounded the thesis that the more economic evolution debars the equitable accumulation of wealth by all individuals, the more government must impose limitations upon the freedom of some individuals. In so doing, he occupied the middle ground between Bentham and Spencer. His doctrine was basically Utilitarian, but it was not in agreement amounting to identity with opinions of the Benthamite tradition. The essential and abiding character of Mill's Utilitarian ethic was socialistic but not utopian; his approach was pragmatic, but it was also too ambitious for the times.

The results he achieved were not exactly dramatic, and at times one may be moved to question whether or not he was successful to any appreciable degree in any of the areas upon which he focused his attention and to which he devoted his most sincere efforts. Sixty times he rose to his feet to deliver a speech or to offer some comment on Gladstone's Reform Bill. One of his finest speeches was delivered on the women's suffrage amendment to this bill. But his cause was defeated by a vote of 123 to 73. His most impassioned speeches in Parliament were on the subject of the Jamaican uprising; yet he not only failed to obtain a conviction of Governor Eyre but was also forced to witness the approval by the House of a measure which reimbursed the governor for his trial expenses. Mill's eloquent pleas on behalf of Ireland produced small results, though they endeared him to the Irishman—no mean accomplishment for an Englishman of that period.

The long-range effects are more flattering to him. When one considers England today—women voting, the influence of the working classes, the distribution of the tax burden, the numerous measures aimed at improving public education, and Eire's independence—it is difficult to deny that Mill's words resounded through the dusty corridors of time.

In his parliamentary messages one may clearly see Mill's blend of acute observation and swift, yet careful, analysis. He had the creative imagination that is sometimes looked upon as the basic characteristic of genius, and he had dynamic energy. It is the combination of these qualities that seems to manifest itself most distinctly in his parliamentary speeches and to which one must attribute much of his ethical appeal.

Ethos, that almost indefinable something that resides within the individual, was clearly one of his most powerful instruments of persuasion. The impression he made upon an audience because of his personal habits, his expressed thoughts, and his actions unquestionably did much to win the support of many who listened to his words. Carlyle, who knew Mill well, describes him as "modest, remarkably gifted with precision of utterance; enthusiastic yet lucid, calm." [24]

Although Bain asserts that the powerful adjunct of wit was hardly within Mill's reach,[25] he had a droll sense of humor and a keen sense of the ridiculous. He had a distinct fondness for really clever humor, and he was quite adept at utilizing it. An example of this is found in a story attributed to him about people who tend to monopolize conversation, one of his particular aversions. He tells of two Frenchmen who were engaged in a heated argument. One was in full possession of the floor, and quite determined to keep it as long as possible. So intent was the other upon breaking in that a third person, watching the contest from the sidelines, observed: "If he spits, he's done." [26] On another occasion, in *The Spirit of the Age,* he reminds his audience that: "To find fault with our ancestors for not having . . . universal suffrage, and vote by ballot, would be like quarreling with the Greeks and Romans for not using steam navigation, when we know it is so safe and expeditious." [27]

Hansard's *Parliamentary Debates* provides a veritable storehouse of epigrammatic expressions which illustrate Mill's facility in the construction of succinct statements with his own brand of delightful jest:

The right of voting may be only the right of being outvoted (April 13, 1866).

. . . .

I did not mean that Conservatives are generally stupid; I meant, that stupid persons are generally Conservative. . . . And I do not see why honest gentlemen should feel that position at all offensive to them; for it insures their being always an extremely powerful party (May 31, 1866).

. . . .

What is commonly called Utopian is something too good to be practicable; but what they [the opposition] appear to favour is too bad to be practicable (March 12, 1868).

There is no doubt that his consistently courteous address and demeanor won favorable response from every quarter. His whole attitude was that of a man who was completely earnest and thoroughly convinced of the righteousness of his cause. The absence of hypocrisy, dissimulation, or falsification to any degree could not be ignored. This, in any man, connotes a strict adherence to truth; a revelation of just what one feels; and an unwillingness to embellish, exaggerate, or to make pretenses of any sort.

Law and liberty, good government and human rights—these were a faith to Mill, a faith he believed in with all the passion and fervor others took to religion. He lived by a creed, the creed of freedom, and with a supreme confidence in the good sense of ordinary man.

Those who read his speeches can scarcely be blind to the kindness he demonstrates toward a just and troubled mankind, the confidence he inspired, and the strength of mind and character that dominated his words. Even in the stronghold of the opposition this faith made itself felt, for Bain assures us that Mill seldom, if ever, lost ground for want of the ability to make himself personally acceptable even to the most difficult assembly.[28] Even in the consideration of those problems or issues regarding which his fund of knowledge was something less than adequate, he was well equipped to serve the House in the capacity of demanding critic.

Although his speeches were generally applauded for their lucidity, there are times when the detailed analysis of a problem, in order to arrive at the logical proof for which he strove, led Mill into tedious exposition. Thus it is that one may find it possible to admire his perspicacity in a particular instance, while still questioning his perspicuity. For the most part, however, we find his speeches reflect not only his power to think according to the rules of logic as he envisioned them—and therefore in an orderly fashion—but also his powers to impress others with the fact that clearness of thought, soundness of reasoning, and freedom from bias were inherent in his arguments, his decisions, his political theories.

Luxuriance of verbal display, whereby the emotions can be aroused with a hurricane's might, was not part of his equipment. He was not an orator in the same sense as the two Pitts, Burke, Brougham, Macaulay, or Disraeli;[29] Mill did exert a certain type of emotional appeal, but just how one may properly describe it challenges the imagination. Contemporary observers such as Bain, Carlyle, and d'Eichthal, have commented on the fact that crude forms of angry passion were entirely missing from Mill's speeches.[30] He never went into a rage; his treatment of opponents was a model of the ethics of controversy. He distrusted emotion for which he could not find a rational basis. Perhaps it is this fact which conciliated the feelings of his audience. He had no use for the chidings, entreaties, reproaches, and excuses that are normally employed by an orator to stir the emotions of his listeners. He did not intersperse his speeches with complaints and insinuations against his opponents, nor did he employ any rhetorical device for the sole purpose of exciting the vulgar mind. There was, in short, no pompous language barren of facts, no wasteful diffusion of emotional power. There was nothing to refute his complete confidence in his belief that to match passionate oratory against good, sound reason is a waste of effort bordering on the absurd.

Insofar as the total effect of his contributions in Parliament is concerned, there seems to be little question but that his influence was enormous. The progress he made toward purifying the social and political controversies of the time from passion and prejudice and introducing moderation and balance in their stead is a service that cannot be too highly praised. James Truslow Adams expresses the historian's belief that "while the swelling tide of democracy, the desire for self determination, and the general change in attitude upon the part of the public and those actively engaged in government, were due in a large measure to a general change in national outlook regarding democratic reforms, credit must be given to the notable leadership of John Stuart Mill." [31]

Gladstone contributes what is probably the most comprehensive evaluation of Mill as a member of Parliament. Speaking as a colleague, he said: "We all knew Mr. Mill's intellectual eminence before he entered Parliament. What his conduct there principally disclosed was his singular moral elevation. . . . Of all the motives, stings, and stimulations that reach men through their egoism in Parliament, no part could move or even touch him. His conduct and his language were a sermon. . . . He had, I think, the good sense and practical tact of politics, together with the highly independent thought of a recluse. I need not tell you that for the sake of the House of Commons at large, I rejoiced in his advent, and deplored his disappearance. He did us all good." [32]

In the election of November, 1868, Mill again stood for Westminster, but this time he was not successful. As in the previous election, he showed little interest in campaigning for the office, and he again refused to spend any of his own money on the campaign. He attributed his defeat to the fact that the Tories had devoted a substantial sum to beat him. Loss of the election was, perhaps, a disappointment, but he had more pleasurable tasks with which to occupy himself.

For some time he had been much interested in revising his father's *Analysis of the Human Mind,* which was an elaborate attempt to provide a psychological explanation for Jeremy Bentham's economic theories. The project had been delayed by his service in the House of Commons. Now he set to work with a great enthusiasm, and the revised text was published in 1869. He immediately turned his attention to his essay on "Theism"—the final section of his *Three Essays on Religion*— a work that had been pushed aside for some years.

CHAPTER 6

Nature, God, and Man

AS a man approaches the close of his life, it is natural for his thoughts to turn toward theological matters. There is no reason to suppose that Mill was an exception. Although he had throughout his life manifested an interest in philosophy of religion, it was not until a scant five years before his death that he completed his most important treatise on the subject—the last part of his *Three Essays on Religion.*

I *Three Essays on Religion*

Taken collectively, the essays can scarcely be looked upon as an antireligion polemic, as some had expected; but they may seem at first blush to propound a series of beliefs that are the very antithesis of religion. On the contrary, much can be said to support them as a convincing, intellectual endorsement of religion.

There are those who insist that Mill could not commit himself to a religious doctrine, that he could not choose any particular doctrine from among the many in Christendom. Such assertions tend to generate much heat, but they provide little illumination. In such a controversy it appears much more constructive and meaningful to view Mill's beliefs in the light of Auguste Comte's religion of humanity; then his defense of his own beliefs becomes quite understandable. The worst that can be said of Mill is that he was a reluctant sceptic, a designation applied to him by Robert Carr in his essay on "The Religious Thought of John Stuart Mill." [1]

Mill possessed a very sensitive moral consciousness. He had a boundless faith in the capacity of the individual to rise above the narrow confines of self-concern and to espouse a belief in the brotherhood of man, if not the fatherhood of God. He stood firm in his belief that man could and would learn to act in obedience to and in conformity with his obligation to the common good, and to accept his responsibilities to society with an unfailing courage and determination born of this knowledge.

Such an eventuality will not derive from theological myth or superstition, nor from metaphysical speculation, but from the enlightened self-interest of the individual. It is contingent upon the indestructibility of a spirituality based on intelligent conviction. From these familiar premises, he ranges far and wide in the essays to examine the various moral ramifications and social consequences of such conviction.

As he grew older, he seems to have become increasingly resigned to the fact that the views he had expressed were unlikely to obtain ready acceptance by a people in an age that was so much given to an almost evangelical belief that everything would work out in the end—without very much effort on the part of anyone. Nevertheless, he maintained an almost Aristotelian faith in man's rational spirit; and he was confident that the profound truths of life were eventually, if not immediately, amenable to logical analysis. He insisted on the necessity for discovering the answers to man's problems, and he refused to agree that any intuitive course could possibly provide a true apprehension of reality. The former is the only principle that should guide man in his search for knowledge and in his resultant control over his own destiny; the latter was not only ineffective and wasteful—it was morally and psychologically wrong.

The three essays on religion were not written as a unit. In fact, the first two, "Nature" and the "Utility of Religion," gradually evolved over several years and were completed about 1858. The third and final essay, "Theism," which was also the last major work completed by Mill, was written in the period from 1868 to 1870. Mrs. Mill's daughter, Helen Taylor, published all three essays in a single volume in 1874, a year after Mill's death.

In the first of these essays, written in 1854, Mill defines nature as a "collective name for all facts, actual and possible, or (to speak more accurately) a name for the mode, partly known to us and partly unknown, in which all things take place."

Problems arise for man when he attempts to relate his thought and his actions to nature. He frequently becomes confused when he seeks to determine what is natural within the complex of his own mental and physical environment. Mill takes great care to explain why an attempt to do what comes naturally is likely to lead to a mode of action that is morally and intellectually undesirable.

He points out that if all actions are done "through and in obedience to some one or many of nature's physical or mental laws," then it is meaningless to assert that a man should strive to follow nature. He will have no choice in the matter. Rather than accept the false logic of this conception of man and nature, each individual should recognize his ability to rise above his environment and, in certain instances, to insure the goodness of nature through his ability to alter or improve on what is natural. One will find that most of the beneficent developments in nature are the product of his own exertions. Conformity to the limitations of nature is sometimes required, but it can be best viewed as cooperation with influences that cannot be opposed. In short, one should strive to improve on that which can be changed in nature, and learn to endure with maximum possible satisfaction that which is immutable.

The second essay, "Utility of Religion," treats the question of religion's contribution to the individual and to society. Mill recognizes that human virtues, such as justice, truth, morality, are commonly ascribed to motives derived directly from religion. He points out, however, that these are learned virtues, almost always taught as an aspect of religious instruction. There is no question that the possession of these virtues is not only desirable but is actually essential if man is to exist as an intelligent social being. It is this very fact which leads Mill to conclude that, as in ancient Greece, there can be a social morality quite apart from religious influences. This can be accomplished by educating people to see virtue as a social duty. Moreover, the obvious amenability of mankind to public opinion and to social pressures also strongly motivates in this direction.

The efficacy of this social morality is illustrated by showing how easily religious obligation can be ignored when it is not reenforced by the pressure of public opinion: "The oaths taken in courts of justice, and any others which, from the manifest importance to society of their being kept, public opinion rigidly enforces, are felt as real and binding obligations. But university oaths and customhouse oaths, though in a religious point of view equally obligatory, are in practice utterly disregarded even by men in other respects honorable."

In "Theism," which is probably the most ambitious of the three essays, Mill applies his intellectual powers to an inquiry into religion and into the existence and attributes of God. There is much to be found in his treatment of the subject that is reminiscent of David Hume's *Dialogues Concerning Natural Religion,* which apparently exerted a great influence on Mill's thinking.

At the very outset, Mill poses two questions for himself: "First, is the theory which refers to the origin of all phenomena of nature to the will of a creator consistent or not with the ascertained results of science? Secondly, assuming it to be consistent, will its proofs bear to be tested by the principles of evidence and canons of belief by which our long experience of scientific inquiry has proved the necessity of being guided?"

Having made an initial assumption that the only consistent concept of God must be one in which he governs the world according to certain invariable laws, Mill immediately moves to an examination of the nature and value of the various evidences of the creation and government of nature by a sovereign will. Three forms of *a priori* argument are delineated for this purpose: argument for a First Cause, argument from the general consent of mankind, and argument from consciousness.

The argument for a First Cause to which everything in the world owes its existence is rejected "because no cause is needed for the existence of that which has no beginning." He agreed completely with Comte that it is useless to inquire into final courses—one should concentrate on concrete evidence. The argument from the general consent of mankind is found untenable because it does not "afford ground for admitting, even as a hypothesis, the origin in an inherent law of the human mind of a fact otherwise so more than sufficiently, so amply, accounted for." Finally, he disposes of the argument from consciousness by showing it to be no more than a mere speculative delusion.

Following this, Mill turns his attention to the *a posteriori* reasoning of the argument from marks of design in nature. This, he maintains, is an argument of true scientific character, wholly grounded on experience, which can be tested against the established canons of induction. This leads him, in due course, to the conclusion that "in the present state of our knowledge the adaptations in nature afford a large balance of probability in favor of creation by intelligence."

Having established the probable existence of God to his own satisfaction, Mill attempts to construct a profile of His personal attributes, and ultimately he visualizes Him as: "A being of great but limited power, how or by what limited we cannot even conjecture; of great, and perhaps unlimited intelligence . . . who desires and pays some regard to the happiness of his creatures, but who seems to have other motives of action which he cares more for, and who can hardly be supposed to have created the universe for that purpose alone."

Mill next reflects upon the immortality of man. He finds the promise of life in a hereafter not without its limitations. There is a strong doubt in his mind concerning the possibility of mankind's existing in a state of perfection in some heavenly realm. This, he feels confident, is a most unlikely eventuality. And, if man is not to spend eternity in an improved form, Mill questions the desirability of an endless life with all of the personal imperfections and limitations of this world. Would it not be preferable, he asks, to live the best life possible, enjoying whatever pleasures and satisfactions our abilities may provide, and find in death a release from toil and trial. Is this not enough to expect?

In conclusion, he offers a few choice observations on the subject of revelation as a religious phenomenon. The most interesting observation to be found in this section concerns Jesus Christ. Mill says He is placed "even in the estimation of those who have no belief in his inspiration, in the very first rank of the men of sublime genius of whom our species can boast."

Though many men have felt the need for such self-analysis and though more than a few have attempted to set forth their thoughts on God and religion, rarely has anyone been able to leave behind a more definitive and closely reasoned spiritual testament. In these three essays Mill said all that he had to say on this most difficult of subjects. It was a fitting finale to an imposing list of literary achievements. But one task remained to be completed: the summing up of the events of his life.

During this same period, 1869-1870, Mill had continued to work on his *Autobiography*. It is quite possible that it will prove to be his most lasting work. Many critics insist that it is the book upon which his reputation as a writer will rest. There is strong evidence to support this prediction. Published first in 1873, it has run through numerous editions and continues to be reprinted at regular intervals. Its continued popularity, while not conclusive, is certainly suggestive of the *Autobiography's* status as a classic of English literature.

II *Autobiography*

Inasmuch as so many observations drawn from the *Autobiography* have been introduced in a more or less chronological order within the general contest of the present work, it will perhaps suffice to present a structural outline at this time. The book is divided into seven chapters, each of which is designed to cover a particular phase of Mill's career. Chapters I and II overlap considerably, the first covering a period from 1806-1819; the second, 1813-1821. Taken together, they encompass his childhood and early education, the moral influences of his youth, and a description of the character and opinions of James Mill. The years 1821-1823, in which the last phase of his quasi-formal education and the beginning of his self-education are discussed, are covered in Chapter III. The chronology continues through Chapter IV (1823-1828), a time of relative calm; Chapter V (1826-1832), a period that began with his mental crisis of which he gives a poignant account as well as of its aftermath; and Chapter VI (1830-1840), a decade in which he began his association with Mrs. Taylor and during which he produced the first of his major works. Chapter VII, the last and the longest chapter, provides a general review of the remainder of his life, 1840-1870, including a valuable commentary on *A System of Logic, Principles of Political Economy, On Liberty, Considerations on Representative Government,* and other literary efforts of consequence. He also mentions his marriage, his professional life, his parliamentary career, and other affairs of a personal nature. It contains what are perhaps the most charming portions of the *Autobiography*.

This rich collection is not only a key to Mill's own thoughts; it is a remarkable window through which one may obtain a panoramic view of the intellectual history of the nineteenth century. There is born from its pages an inspiring confidence in and admiration for a man who was undoubtedly one of the most important philosophers of his age, a man who exerted an influence that earned for him a position of academic authority and the leadership of a substantial group of practical economists and political scientists. Few readers will deny that the *Autobiography* fulfills the purpose for which it was written —the purpose Mill announces at the very beginning of Chapter I:

I do not for a moment imagine that any part of what I have to relate can be interesting to the public as a narrative, or as being connected with myself. But I have thought . . . it may be useful that there should be some record of an education which was unusual and remarkable, and which, whatever it may have done, has proved how much more than is commonly supposed may be taught, and well taught, in those early years which, in the common modes of what is called instruction, are little better than wasted. It has also seemed to me that in an age of transition in opinions, there may be somewhat both of interest and of benefit in noting the successive phases of any mind which was always pressing forward, equally ready to learn and to unlearn either from its own thoughts or from those of others. But a motive which weighs more with me than either of these, is a desire to make acknowledgement of the debts which my intellectual and moral development owes to other persons; some of them of recognized eminence, others less known than they deserve to be, and the one to whom most of all is due, one whom the world had no opportunity of knowing. The reader whom these things do not interest, has only himself to blame if he reads farther, and I do not desire any further indulgence from him than that of bearing in mind, that for him these pages were not written.

The *Autobiography* is, in many respects, the most remarkable work of its kind in the history of English literature. It lacks the glow and intensity of high-wrought emotion and the poignancy usually associated with such personal reflection, so much preferred by many literary critics. On the other hand, it does possess, in great abundance, other marks of distinction which are basic elements of all great writing. Coupled with this is Mill's special brand of eloquence which has consistently earned the thoroughgoing admiration of discriminating reviewers. He served himself well as his own Boswell.

A book of manifest authority, it is unequaled as a detailed, firsthand statement of actual events and conditions determinative of the course of one man's intellectual development. When this man is the possessor of one of the greatest intellects in the history of ideas, the revelation of what he feels and thinks as his life unfolds is eminently worthy of special consideration. Moreover, the patient reader will discover that this is a not unattractive account; it possesses a distinctive charm. It is not an exciting book, but it is intrinsically interesting. Mill's candor and capacity for detachment is fascinating. Never has a man studied himself with less subjective sentiment or greater humility.

The essential nature of the *Autobiography* understandably imposes certain limitations in point of view, and it allows for honest differences of interpretation of events and influences. Nevertheless, Mill achieves a measure of discrimination and discernment of values in making his choice of particulars. His thoughts flow freely and clearly with scrupulous honesty. Nowhere can there be found that single discordant note that might give rise to suspicion of hypocrisy, dissimulation, or deliberate falsification. The clearly manifest freedom from artificiality or from straining for effect endow the work with a perfection so unobtrusive that the perspicuity and perspicacity of the author are sometimes underestimated.

III *Peroration*

The rostra had served him well, but as his life drew to a close Mill sought literary repose rather than oratorical exercise. He had received an invitation to undertake a lecture tour in the United States, but he declined it.[2] Although the promise of financial reward was attractive, he was more interested in completing his writing. He did return briefly to the public platform in 1871, when he delivered a speech at an organizational meeting and first public hearing of the Land Tenure Reform Association at Freemason's Hall.[3] The views which he expressed concerning the aims and objectives of the association reiterate his Utilitarian principle regarding the acquisition of private property and the responsibility of the government to facilitate and safeguard the property rights of the individual. The last of Mill's speeches, also on the subject of Land Tenure Reform, was presented at Exeter Hall on March 18, 1873. In it he continued the theme developed in his previous address and presents the arguments set forth in his article "Advice to Land Reformers," published in the *Examiner* a short time earlier.[4] It was, in substance, a page from the *Principles of Political Economy*.[5]

This speech was a fitting conclusion to his public career. It was characterized by a directness of thought and lucidity of style unsurpassed in any of his previous speeches. It possessed a fervor which suggests an increasing awareness that his life, which was already long, could not much longer sustain the battle he had waged against physical oppression for so many years. Perhaps he sensed that this was to be his final discourse. The London *Times*, in reporting the event,[6] commented on the great interest created by his reappearance, which was received with loud cheers from his audience.[7] It was the last time that his voice was to be heard in public debate. In less than two months the greatest spokesman of Utilitarianism would be stilled forever.

Seventeen years had passed since he had been told that he had consumption and that his days were numbered. Now, in 1872, sixty-seven years old, he seemed to be in quite good health and high spirits, and he was indefatigable in his work. He was enjoying renewed fame and popularity as a result of the seventh edition of the *Principles of Political Economy*, published in 1871; and a revised edition, the eighth, of *A System of Logic*, which appeared in 1872.

As 1873 approached he began to grow weary, and he looked forward to the mental and spiritual refreshment of a sojourn at his house in Avignon. When spring approached he set his affairs in England in order and prepared to cross the Channel. He arrived in Avignon in April, happy to be back and eager to relax in the warm atmosphere that he and Harriet had so much enjoyed. His days were filled with happy memories as he walked daily along the paths of the familiar countryside. It was a period of peace and freedom from intellectual activity such as he had rarely allowed himself.

One morning, early in May, he set out on a long walk through the countryside. It was a beautiful day, and he may have overexerted himself. When he returned, he was in fine spirits. That evening he developed a fever. The following day his condition rapidly grew more serious. On May 7, 1873 he died; the next day he was buried beside Harriet. His work was done. It now remained for others to determine how well it had been done.

IV *L'envoi*

Few things in this world are more difficult to evaluate than the influence of a writer. And if the writer happens to be a serious philosopher, the difficulties are compounded; if he is a political philosopher, they defy description. This is particularly true of John Stuart Mill.

The consentient testimony of critical scholars has been consistently clouded by an understandable but unfortunate uncertainty. There is agreement only in the belief that the impact of his words must be interpreted in the light of permanent principles that have survived the test of practical application.

Although he is more often thought of as a literary figure than as an orator, his collected speeches reveal that he was a consummate rhetorician in the full sense of the term.[8] The speeches possess the same characteristics which are apparent in his written works. In his speaking as in his writing he refused to mistake volubility for rhetorical excellence; he conscientiously avoided loading his speeches or his written work with dogma to be believed on faith; he consistently presented ideas and principles which he expected to be apprehended. Mill never harbored any desire to think for men, but he was utterly devoted to the task of discovering means whereby they might be encouraged and enabled to think for themselves. He scorned the clever rhetorical legerdemain to which he alludes in *The*

Spirit of the Age as "the art of appearing profoundly versed in a subject to those who know nothing about it." [9] As his friend Bain remarked, his speeches possessed "all the qualities of his published works; that is to say, original in thought, powerfully reasoned." [10] There seems to be no question that his speeches, in both form and content, were nearly as important as his written works. An examination of his parliamentary addresses should remove any doubt of this.

Unfriendly critics may asseverate that Mill looked upon his term in the House of Commons as little more than an exercise in the art of democratic debate and that his influence withered as a result of his performance in the realm of practical politics. It is quite possible that no man was less versed in the devious arts of the professional politician. It is highly probable that no politician was ever better versed in the theory of government. While it is true that the measures he supported in the House frequently went down to defeat, it is equally true that such failure was only relative and that there are elements of permanence in the legislative record. His clearly manifest dedication to the cause of freedom and justice and his ability to expound human and social problems are certainly part of his parliamentary memorial. His debates in Parliament gave voice to the broad body of doctrine embodied in his written works, and these concepts entitle him to rank as a major political figure.

A much more definitive assessment can be made of his literary characteristics. In most of his published works, Mill was primarily concerned with expounding difficult philosophical concepts. The result was usually a happy and effective collaboration of logic and linguistic facility. His style was functional and not particularly elegant or charming in the usual literary sense. Although his works are not devoid of neatly turned phrases or of skillfully drawn illustrations and allusions, he did not invest them with a great deal of highly imaginative metaphor, and memorable purple patches are few in number. There are numerous instances in which the complex pattern of his thoughts is difficult for any but the most disciplined minds to follow. His paragraphs are at times too diffused, and some of his sentences can be construed only with painstaking effort. Certain peculiarities of grammar frequently served to make his style heavy and, on occasion, obscure.[11]

There are those who would maintain that because of these adverse elements found in his works, Mill is not strictly speaking a literary figure at all. They somehow feel that these defects prevent him from providing his thoughts with sufficient emotional quality. Such critics demonstrate a remarkable lack of understanding and appreciation of the multifaceted nature of expository writing. And Mill was primarily—perhaps one should say exclusively—an expository writer. Not even in his personal correspondence could he keep entirely aloof from exposition. And exposition, in its typical character, embodies clear statement and adequate exemplification of principle. The adverse effect of involved grammatical structure and somewhat shattered syntax may give pain to grammarians, but this was not sufficient to detract seriously from the power of expression with which his remarkable polemical aptitude endowed him. His great strength was not a matter of mere style: "it lay more in his command of thought, and in his tact in discerning what would suit the persons addressed. When he set himself to argue a point, his information and command of principles usually enabled him to exhaust his case." [12]

In the final analysis, after the opinions of both grammarians and historians have been weighed in the balance, what remains to be said? Mill's major works are frequently quoted, but they are seldom read in their entirety outside of university walls. The *Autobiography, Logic, Liberty,* and *Utilitarianism* are reprinted from time to time, and are not difficult to obtain. Most of his articles and virtually all of his speeches have been ignored except by the more scholarly researchers. The measure of his contribution to English letters and philosophy, however, transcends the popularity of his books or the praise of his academic admirers.

The ultimate measure of his unique contribution is the continued ability of his ideas to penetrate the minds of men and to sway opinion. Today, as in Mill's day, man strives to reach new realms of human solidarity and social peace. The extent to which the means of accomplishing this end have their genesis in John Stuart Mill no one can say. But his words continue to have a fermenting effect on social, political, and economic theory. He has served truth, and for this he is held in grateful memory by all who share his great love and concern for mankind.

As Elihu Root once observed, "true love of country is not mere blind partisanship. It is regard for the people of one's country and all of them." There is hardly a more apt description of Mill's concern for mankind. One wishes that there were more persons in the world today who would share this sentiment, men and women who would demonstrate this belief in their words and actions as Mill did. It may be that the terror of the times has imbued people with a fatalism that carries with it the seed of destruction. The same might be said for the Victorian era.

Be this as it may, there is much to be said for the value of Mill's works aside from their literary merit. Only the most naïve can read them as curios of a Victorian intellectual. The conscientious reader will find himself brought up short again and again by Mill's amazing gift of prophecy as much as by his diagnostic acumen. Very few of the serious authors of his day have been able to provide us with a more discriminating synthesis of nineteenth century ideas; few can provide us with so many ideas that are of genuine significance in the political and economic debates of the twentieth century.

Almost two hundred years have passed since Jeremy Bentham published his *Fragments on Government* and his *Introduction to Principles of Morals and Legislation;*[13] almost a century has passed since Mill completed his major adaptations and expansion of Bentham's ideas. There are still places in the world that are paradise for the privileged and purgatory for the underprivileged; men continue to assail the stupidity of the masses and the self-satisfaction of the few. But progress and reform have been clearly and continuously manifest throughout a substantial portion of the world.

Each day men receive fresh reminders of Mill's warning that subjugation can become a state of mind, that liberty must not remain an abstraction and cannot exist in the absence of power to use it. Men continue to be faced with the difficult problem of drawing a demonstrable connection between the forms of government and the character of a people.

In the midst of this cosmos or, if one prefers, chaos, it is refreshing and encouraging, and sometimes ironic, to find Mill's intellectual power still exerting a positive influence in the most unlikely quarters. Among the intellectuals in the Soviet Union there are still some who hopefully read Strakhov's Russian translation of *The Subjection of Women;* in the China of Mao Tse-tung there are those who continue to admire Yen Fu, translator of *On Liberty* into Chinese; in the most remote corners of the world there can be found those who have learned from Mill to recognize man's obligation to humanity. This was Mill's first principle. He did not create it; he did not discover it; he awakened it. This, in his own time as in the twentieth century, was his great contribution to mankind.

Notes and References

Chapter One

1. See F. A. Hayek, *John Stuart Mill and Harriet Taylor: Their Correspondence and Subsequent Marriage* (Chicago, 1951), Appendix III, p. 280 for Mill Family Tree.

2. John Stuart Mill, *Autobiography*, The World's Classics Edition, Oxford University Press (London, 1949), pp. 4-72.

3. *Ibid.*, pp. 60-61.

4. John Stuart Mill, *The Spirit of the Age* (Chicago, 1942), pp. 66-68.

5. Alexander Bain, *John Stuart Mill: A Criticism* (London, 1882), p. 22.

6. *Ibid.*, p. 25.

7. Mill, *Autobiography, op. cit.*, pp. 104-05.

8. *Ibid.*, p. 105.

9. *Ibid.*, p. 106.

10. *Ibid.*, p. 108.

11. *Ibid.*, p. 132.

12. *Ibid.*, p. 123.

13. *Revue Historique*, "John Stuart Mill, Correspondence Inedite avec Gustave d'Eichthal" (Paris, 1902), Vol. LXXIV, p. vi.

14. Published as an appendix to the *Autobiography, op. cit.*, pp. 267-74.

15. Mill, *Autobiography, op. cit.*, p. 67.

16. John Stuart Mill, *Utilitarianism, Liberty and Representative Government*, Everyman's Library (London, 1940), p. 9.

17. Two of these were published in the *Journal of Adult Education* (London), Vol. IV, No. 1, October, 1929, pp. 38-48; the third appeared in the *Archiv fur Sozialwissenschaft und Sozialpolitik*, Verlag von J. C. Mohr, 62 Bond, Turbruzen, 1929, pp. 225-39.

18. Thomas Robert Malthus (1766-1834), an English political economist who contended that population increases faster than the means of subsistence, and it must be checked by social and moral restraints. His ideas are set forth in his *Essay on Population*.

19. Adam Smith (1723-1790), a Scottish political economist and

author of *The Wealth of Nations*. He also wrote the *Theory of Moral Sentiments* in which he sought to establish sympathy as the basis of morality.

20. Published in *Economics*, V., March, 1925, pp. 1-6.

21. Alexander Carlyle, ed., *Letters of Thomas Carlyle to John Stuart Mill, John Sterling and Robert Browning* (London, 1923), p. vi.

22. The first speech was printed as an appendix to the *Autobiography, op. cit.*, pp. 275-87; the second appeared in the *Archiv fur Sozialwissenschaft und Sozialpolitik, op. cit.*, pp. 460-66.

23. Mephistopheles was depicted in Goethe's *Faust* as a sardonic, scoffing fellow.

24. Published in the *Archiv fur Sozialwissenschaft und Sozialpolitik, op. cit.*, pp. 239-50.

25. Published in the *Archiv fur Sozialwissenschaft und Sozialpolitik, op. cit.*, pp. 449-60.

26. Published as an appendix to the *Autobiography, op. cit.*, pp. 288-99.

27. Elie Halevy, *The Liberal Awakening* (New York, 1949), p. 189.

28. Both speeches were published in the *Autobiography, op. cit.*, pp. 300-25.

29. John Sterling (1806-1844), a close friend of Samuel Coleridge and Thomas Carlyle. The latter was author of his biography.

30. Montesquieu, Charles Louis de Secondat, Baron de la Brède et de Montesquieu (1689-1755), a French philosophical writer on government and history. He is best known for his work *L'Ésprit de Lois*.

31. Compare letter to John Sterling, dated April 15, 1829, in Elliot's *The Letters of John Stuart Mill* (London, 1910), Vol. I, 1, which seems to arise out of this speech.

32. Published as an appendix to the *Autobiography, op. cit.*, pp. 310-25.

33. Mill, *Autobiography, op. cit.*, p. 89.

34. A. W. Levi, "The Mental Crisis of John Stuart Mill," *The Psychoanalytical Review* (New York, 1945), Vol. XXXII, 98.

35. J. A. Froude, *Thomas Carlyle, The First Forty Years* (1882 Edition), Vol. II, 190.

36. William Leonard Courtney, *The Life of John Stuart Mill* (London, 1889), p. 71.

37. Bain, *op. cit.*, p. 191.

38. Trudy Bliss (ed.), *Jane Welsh Carlyle: A New Selection of Her Letters,* (London, 1950), p. 89.

39. Mill, *Autobiography, op. cit.*, p. 89.

40. Although Mill never pardoned Roebuck for his interference, the latter remained a great admirer. Thirty years later, when Mill was elected to the House of Commons, Roebuck did everything in his power to assist and support him. There is some indication that, in later years, Mill responded in some degree to the memories of their earlier friendship.

41. Adultery and brutality were the only grounds for divorce; the father retained custody of the children; remarriage required a special Act of Parliament.

42. *Jane Welsh Carlyle Letters, op. cit.*, p. 59.

43. F. A. Hayek, *John Stuart Mill and Harriet Taylor: Their Correspondence and Subsequent Marriage* (Chicago, 1951), p. 169.

44. Mill, *Autobiography, op. cit.*, p. 36.

45. *The Letters of John Stuart Mill, op. cit.*, Vol. II, 134.

46. John Stuart Mill, *Three Essays on Religion* (London, 1874), p. 174.

47. Mill, *Autobiography, op. cit.*, p. 33.

48. Mill, *Three Essays on Religion, op. cit.*, pp. 254-55.

49. Mill, *Autobiography, op. cit.*, pp. 156-60, 203-08.

50. Hayek, *op. cit.*, p. 178.

51. Mill, *Autobiography, op. cit.*, p. 207.

52. *Ibid.*, pp. 124-29.

53. *Ibid.*, pp. 40-41.

54. *Ibid.*, pp. 172-73.

55. Hayek, *op. cit.*, p. 149 and Note.

56. March 31, 1849.

57. September 18, 1844.

58. See *The Life of John Stuart Mill* (New York, 1954), by Michael St. John Packe, for an excellent account of this whole affair.

Chapter Two

1. Mill, *Autobiography, op. cit.*, pp. 169-87.

2. Clara, Jane, and Mary subsequently married; Harriet remained single and maintained a home for their mother until Mrs. Mill's death in 1854.

3. Herbert Taylor was born in 1827; Algernon, in 1830; Helen, in 1831.

4. George Mill, who was dying from tuberculosis, hastened the process by committing suicide in 1852; Mrs. Mill died of cancer in 1854.

5. Hayek, *op. cit.*, pp. 171-81, 207.

6. Mill, *Autobiography, op. cit.*, p. 3.

7. *Morning Chronicle*, August 28, 1851.

8. 1840.

9. Mill, *Autobiography, op. cit.*, pp. 177-78.

10. Alexander Bain assisted in the proofreading and rewriting.

11. William Whewell, D.D., quondam Cambridge Professor of Moral Philosophy.

12. Sir William Hamilton owed much of his reputation as a philosopher to these works and his treatise, *The Philosophy of Perception.* Mill subsequently criticized Hamilton severely for his espousal of intuition as a source of knowledge.

13. *The Letters of John Stuart Mill, op. cit.*, Vol. I, 116.

14. Richard Paul Anschutz, *The Philosophy of John Stuart Mill,* (London, 1953) p. 125.

15. He was especially influenced by Bentham, Saint-Simon, Comte, Bacon, and Hume.

16. Whittaker, *Comte and Mill,* p. 60.

17. Mill, *Autobiography, op. cit.*, p. 188.

18. *Ibid.*, p. 199.

19. Written 1830-1831.

20. Mill, *Autobiography, op. cit.*, p. 152.

21. Mill, *Principles of Political Economy* (London, 1904), p. 1, Preliminary Remarks.

22. *Ibid.*, p. 590.

23. Compare Adam Smith, *The Wealth of Nations,* 1776; David Ricardo, *Principles of Political Economy and Taxation,* 1817.

24. Mill, *Principles of Political Economy, op. cit.*, Book V, Chap. IX, p. 590.

25. *Ibid.*, Book II, Chap. I, p. 127.

26. In the period from 1841 to 1850, the United States received 780, 719 Irish immigrants.

27. Mill, *Utilitarianism, Liberty and Representative Government, op. cit.*, p. 72.

28. *Ibid.*, p. 75.

29. Compare *The Saint Andrews Inaugural Address.*

30. Mill, *On Liberty, op. cit.*, pp. 79, 95.

31. *Ibid.*, pp. 89, 107.

32. *Ibid.*, p. 114.

33. *Ibid.*, pp. 134, 138, 140.

34. *Ibid.*, pp. 149-50.

35. Mill, *Autobiography, op. cit.*, pp. 218-19.

Chapter Three

1. Mill, *Utilitarianism, Liberty and Representative Government, op. cit.*, p. 175.

2. *Ibid.*, p. 177.

3. *Ibid.*, pp. 185, 188.
4. *Ibid.*, p. 193.
5. *Ibid.*, p. 208.
6. *Ibid.*, p. 218.
7. *Ibid.*, p. 228.
8. *Ibid.*, p. 241.
9. *Ibid.*, p. 243.
10. *Ibid.*, p. 248.
11. *Ibid.*, pp. 256-57.
12. *Ibid.*, pp. 312-13.
13. *Ibid.*, p. 335.
14. *Ibid.*, pp. 347-56.
15. *Ibid.*, p. 359.
16. *Ibid.*, pp. 359-60, 364.
17. Compare *Liberty*, pp. 66-67.
18. Mill, *Autobiography, op. cit.*, pp. 230-35.
19. *Ibid.*, pp. 235-36.

Chapter Four

1. John Maynard Keynes, *The General Theory of Employment, Interest and Money* (New York, 1936), p. 383.
2. See *Lettres Inedites de John Stuart Mill a Auguste Comte,* ed. Levy-Bruhl (Paris, 1899), p. 549 (May 17, 1847).
3. The term Utilitarian was adopted by Mill from Galt's *Annals of the Parish.* See *Autobiography, op. cit.*, pp. 151-52, 226.
4. Carlyle referred to this as the "Profit-and-Loss Philosophy," which maintained that Soul is synonymous with Stomach. See T. Carlyle, *Sartor Resartus* (New York, 1937), p. 159.
5. Mill, *Utilitarianism, Liberty and Representative Government, op. cit.*, p. 15.
6. Apropos of Mill's general attitude on this subject, he reportedly commented that "in America the life of one sex is devoted to dollar hunting, and of the other to breeding dollar hunters." I have been unable to document this, and the quotation marks are arbitrary.
7. Mill, *Utilitarianism, Liberty and Representative Government, op. cit.*, p. 60.
8. Mill, *Autobiography, op. cit*, pp. 151-52.
9. Mill, *Utilitarianism, Liberty and Representative Government, op. cit.*, p. 25.
10. *Ibid.*, pp. 40-41.
11. *Ibid.*, pp. 54-55.
12. *Ibid.*, pp. 226-29.
13. June 29, 1864.

14. July 1, 1864.

15. John Bright, British Quaker, reformer, statesman; served in the House of Commons and in Gladstone's cabinet.

16. See Wendell Phillips Garrison, *William Lloyd Garrison* (New York, 1894), Vol. IV, 211-13, and Mill's *Autobiography, op. cit.*, p. 227.

17. The text of the speech is contained in an anthology edited by Mayo W. Hazeltine, *Orations from Homer to William McKinley* (New York, 1902), pp. 6183-85.

18. Saint Andrews University is the oldest Scottish University. It was founded in 1411, and in Great Britain only Oxford (1160) and Cambridge (1217) are older.

19. February 9, 1867.

20. January-April 1867, Vol. CXXVII, 131.

21. January-April 1867, Vol. VIII, 505.

22. Published as an appendix to the *Autobiography, op. cit.*, pp. 326-30.

23. Mill, *Dissertations and Discussions* (New York, 1882), pp. 238-54.

24. Mill, *Inaugural Address at the University of Saint Andrews,* (Boston, 1867), p. 7.

Chapter Five

1. Compare Speech on "Representation of the People," delivered in the House of Commons, June 27, 1867.

2. Mill, *Autobiography, op. cit.*, p. 240.

3. *Ibid.*, pp. 240-41.

4. Cincinnatus, it will be recalled, was a Roman who was summoned from his farm to serve as Imperator. He defeated the enemies of Rome, resigned his dictatorship, and returned to his farm.

5. The Reform Bill of 1832 resulted from the pressure of the working class, but it was the middle class who benefited from the bill by obtaining the franchise. The number of voters increased, but the majority of the adult males still failed to meet the property qualifications.

6. He spoke on the Reform Bill of 1866 on April 13, May 31, and July 17. Subsequently speeches on May 9, 17, 20, 30; June 27; and July 5, 1867, were delivered on the Reform Bill of that year, which was ultimately passed by the House of Commons.

7. April 13, 1866.

8. Elliot, *op. cit.*, Vol. II, 59-60.

9. *Westminster Review,* New Series, Vol. XXXIV, July, 1868, 218-19.

10. The London *Times,* June 1, 1866.

11. Mill's plea for women suffrage was to go unanswered for many years. It was not until 1918 that England granted the franchise to women over thirty. In 1928 the qualifying age for women was reduced to twenty-one.

12. April 17, 1866.

13. January 13, 1846.

14. *Parliamentary Papers*, 1852, IX, 284-95.

15. May 17, 1866.

16. Mill, *Autobiography, op. cit.*, p. 248.

17. *Ibid.*, p. 253.

18. Emery Neff, *Carlyle and Mill, Mystic and Utilitarian* (New York, 1924), p. 40.

19. July 24, 1866.

20. August 4, 1866.

21. Thomas Hare proposed that the nation be divided into small districts approximately equal in population, each of which would have two or more candidates as representatives. In order to be elected, the candidate would have to receive as many votes as the total number of votes cast divided by the number of representations allocated to the district.

22. March 27, 1868.

23. *Westminster Review,* New Series, Vol. XXXV (April, 1868), 429-30.

24. Alexander Carlyle, ed., *Letters of Thomas Carlyle to John Stuart Mill, John Sterling and Robert Browning* (London, 1923), p. v.

25. Bain, *op. cit.*, p. 185.

26. *Ibid.*, p. 189.

27. Mill, *The Spirit of the Age, op. cit.*, p. 48.

28. Bain, *op. cit.*, p. 184.

29. *Ibid.*, p. 184.

30. *Ibid.*, p. 151.

31. James Truslow Adams, *Empire of the Seven Seas: The British Empire* (London, 1940), p. 128.

32. Courtney, *op. cit.*, p. 141.

Chapter Six

1. *Journal of History of Ideas,* October-December, 1962.

2. It is reported that the American Social Science Association offered to pay all expenses for Mill and an escort during his visit in the United States, and to pay a stipend of $300 for each speech he delivered.

3. The speech is included in *Dissertations and Discussions, op. cit.*, pp. 238-54.

4. The *Examiner*, January 4, 1873, pp. 1-2.

5. Mill, *Principles of Political Economy, op. cit.*, Bk. II, Chap. 2, pp. 133-45.

6. March 19, 1873.

7. The speech is included in *Dissertations and Discussions, op. cit.*, pp. 269-78.

8. John B. Ellery, "The Collected Speeches of John Stuart Mill, With Introduction and Notes," University of Wisconsin, Ph.D. Dissertation, 1954.

9. Mill, *Spirit of the Age, op. cit.*, p. 46.

10. Bain, *op. cit.*, p. 125.

11. *Ibid.*, pp. 175-76.

12. *Ibid.*, p. 184.

13. 1776 and 1789 respectively.

Selected Bibliography

PRIMARY SOURCES

The Spirit of the Age. Edited by F. A. Hayek. Chicago: University of Chicago Press, 1942.

A System of Logic. London: Longmans, Green and Co., 1930.

Essays on Some Unsettled Questions of Political Economy. London: London School of Economics, 1949.

Principles of Political Economy. London: Longmans, Green and Co., 1904.

Dissertations and Discussions. Boston: W. V. Spencer, 1875.

Considerations on Representative Government. Edited by Currin V. Shields. New York: Liberal Arts Press, 1958.

Utilitarianism, Liberty and Representative Government. Introduction by A. D. Lindsay. Everyman's Library, New York: E. P. Dutton and Co., 1950.

Auguste Comte and Positivism. Boston: W. V. Spencer, 1865.

An Examination of Sir William Hamilton's Philosophy. Boston: W. V. Spencer, 1865.

The Subjugation of Women. New York: E. P. Dutton and Co., 1955.

Autobiography. The World's Classics Edition, London: Oxford University Press, 1949.

Inaugural Address at the University of Saint Andrews. Boston: Littell, Gay and Company, 1867.

Three Essays on Religion. London: Longmans, Green and Co., 1874.

The Letters of John Stuart Mill. Edited by Hugh S. R. Elliot. London: Longmans, Green and Co., 1910.

SECONDARY SOURCES

This is a selective list only of the booklength studies in English of John Stuart Mill. Titles of books are listed here only if they have a considerable value. Additional references of interest are contained in the notes.

Albee, Ernest. *A History of English Utilitarianism.* London: Macmillan Co., 1902. Throws light on the intellectual milieu in which Mill developed his Utilitarian theories and serves as a useful introduction to figures of importance in the movement.

Anschutz, Richard Paul. *The Philosophy of John Stuart Mill.* London: Oxford University Press, 1953. An important philosophical treatment and critical estimate of Mill's work.

Bain, Alexander. *John Stuart Mill: A Criticism.* London: Henry Holt and Co., 1882. A firsthand report by a personal friend of Mill, and an interesting critical estimate of his works.

Bliss, Trudy, ed. *Jane Welsh Carlyle: A New Selection of Her Letters.* London: Victor Gollancz, Ltd., 1950. A sensitive and detailed chronicle that provides a delightful view of Mill's social environment.

Crawford, John Forsyth. *The Relation of Inference to Fact in Mill's Logic.* Chicago: University of Chicago Press, 1916. A profound, penetrating examination of an essential aspect of the *Logic.*

Davidson, William L. *Political Thought in England: The Utilitarians from Bentham to Mill.* London: Oxford University Press, 1915. An excellent critical study of the political panorama against which Utilitarianism came into being. Very helpful in tracing the development of Mill's concepts.

Ellery, John B. "The Collected Speeches of John Stuart Mill, With Introduction and Notes." University of Wisconsin, Ph.D. Dissertation, 1954. A record of Mill's speeches, including a critical commentary on his rhetoric.

Halevy, Elie. *The Growth of Philosophic Radicalism.* London: Macmillan Co., 1928. An extensive and intelligent review that establishes the background of Mill's political philosophy and presents a constructive evaluation of its significance.

Hansard. *Parliamentary Debates, 1865-1868.* London: Cornelius Bush. Third series, commencing with the accession of William IV, Volume CLXXXI.

Hayek, F. A. *John Stuart Mill and Harriet Taylor: Their Correspondence and Subsequent Marriage.* Chicago: University of Chicago Press, 1951. A carefully edited collection of letters which provide much insight into the personal and social life of Mill and Mrs. Taylor.

Jackson, Reginald. *An Examination of the Deductive Logic of John Stuart Mill.* London: Oxford University Press, 1951. Somewhat technical, but a comprehensive and capable treatment of the subject.

Laski, Harold, ed. *The Autobiography of John Stuart Mill.* London: Oxford University Press, 1924. Contains an excellent introduction by the editor, and includes the text of six of Mill's speeches: "The Utility of Knowledge," "The British Constitution," "Perfectibility," "Notes of Speech Against Sterling," "The Church," and "Secular Education."

MacMinn, Ney, with J. R. Hainds and James McNab McCrimmon, eds. *Bibliography of the Published Writings of John Stuart Mill.* Evanston: Northwestern University Press, Northwestern University Studies in the Humanities, No. 12, 1945. Accurate, extensive inventory essential for a thorough study of Mill.

Neff, Emery. *Carlyle and Mill, Mystic and Utilitarian.* New York: Columbia University Press, 1924. A helpful examination of the two men and their influence upon each other and upon their age.

Nesbitt, George L. *Benthamite Reviewing.* New York: Columbia University Press, 1934. Contains an outstanding commentary on the *Westminster Review,* which published a number of Mill's articles and which he later owned and edited.

Packe, Michael St. John. *The Life of John Stuart Mill.* New York: Macmillan Co., 1954. Undoubtedly the finest biography of Mill.

Tawney, Guy Allen. *John Stuart Mill's Theory of Inductive Logic.* Cincinnati: University of Cincinnati Press, 1905. A careful study and a valuable source from which to obtain an overall view of the subject.

Index

Index

Mill, Clara, 47, 121
Mill, George, 45-47, 121
Mill, Harriet (sister), 121
Mill, Henry, 45
Mill, James, 19, 22, 34, 40, 48, 75, 77, 81, 87; *Analysis of the Human Mind*, 103
Mill, Mrs. James, 46, 48; *see also* Burrow, Harriet
Mill, James (brother), 45-47
Mill, Jane, 121
Mill, John Stuart (*see also* Chronology, 13-14): birth, 19; education, 20-21; reads law, 22; joins East India Company, 22; first articles, 22; debating society speeches, 23-27; sense of humor, 24, 100-1; ethics, 27, 33-36; mental crisis, 28-30; appearance, 30-31; meets Harriet Taylor, 30; marriage, 33; religion, 34; editor, 39; literary criticism, 39; death of father, 40; publisher, 41; family quarrel, 46-48; death of mother, 46, 48; promotion and retirement from India House, 31, 49, 88; death of wife, 49; logic, 51; Rector of Saint Andrews, 82; Doctor of Laws, 85; elected to House of Commons, 90; oratory, 100-3; defeated in election, 103; death, 113; style, 114

WORKS
"Advice to Land Reformers," 112
An Examination of Sir William Hamilton's Philosophy, 72
Autobiography, 23, 28, 36, 40, 43, 46, 49, 74, 95, 109-11, 115
"August Comte and Positivism," 72
"Coalition Government, The," 26
Considerations on Representative Government, 50, 64-73, 110
"Contest in America, The," 83
Dissertations and Discussions, 36, 50, 62
"Influence of the Aristocracy, The," 26

"Influence of Lawyers, The," 24
"Nature," 105-6
On Liberty, 25, 50, 58-62, 63, 65, 73, 110, 115, 116
"On the Church," 27
"Perfectibility," 26
Principles of Political Economy, 36-37, 44, 54-58, 89, 110, 112
Saint Andrews Inaugural Address, 84-87
Some Unsettled Questions of Political Economy, 38-54
Spirit of the Age, The, 20, 37-38, 101, 113-14
Subjection of Women, The, 63, 117
System of Logic, 36, 41, 50-54, 63, 110, 112, 115
"Theism," 105, 107-9
Thoughts on Parliamentary Reform, 48, 50, 61, 91
Three Essays on Religion, 86-87, 103-9
Tribute to William Lloyd Garrison, 82-84
Utilitarianism, 50, 65, 75-82, 115
"Utility of Knowledge," 24
"Utility of Religion," 105, 106-7
Mill, Mrs. John Stuart, *see* Taylor, Harriet
Mill, Mary (Colman), 46, 121
Milton, John, 20
Montesquieu, Baron de, 27, 60, 120
Monthly Repository, 38, 62
Morning Chronicle, 22, 94

Napoleon III, 58
New England Society, 84

Opium War, 43
Ovid, 20
Owenites Cooperative Society, 23
Oxford University, 74

Palmerston, Lord, 71, 93
Paris, 63
Parliamentary History and Review, 28
Peel, Sir Robert, 26

Index

92
Mill